The Church
in the *Life*
of the
Black Family

The
CHURCH
in the
LIFE of the
BLACK
FAMILY

Wallace Charles Smith

Judson Press® Valley Forge

THE CHURCH IN THE LIFE OF THE BLACK FAMILY
Copyright ©1985
Judson Press, Valley Forge, PA 19482-0851
Fifth Printing, 1993

Unless otherwise indicated, Bible quotations in this volume are from the New American Standard Bible, © The Lockman Foundation 1960, 1962, 1963, 1968, 1971, 1972, 1973, 1975, and used by permission.
Other quotations of the Bible are from the Revised Standard Version of the Bible copyrighted 1946, 1952 © 1971, 1973 by the Division of Christian Education of the National Council of the Churches of Christ in the U.S.A., and used by permission.

Library of Congress Cataloging-in-Publication Data
Smith, Wallace Charles.
  The church in the life of the black family.

  (Judson family life series)
  Bibliography: p.
  1. Afro-American families—Religious life.
I. Title.   II. Series.
BR563.N4S575   1985   208'.996073   85-24186
ISBN 0-8170-1040-8

Editors' Foreword

THE CHURCH IN THE LIFE OF THE BLACK FAMILY by Wallace Charles Smith, in our opinion, is a landmark volume. It is the first book written by and containing the germinal thinking of this outstanding young pastor/scholar. It is unique in its approach in illuminating the relationship of the black church to its families.

This book is one of a series of books being published by Judson Press on marriage and family for contemporary Christians. The purposes of the Judson Family Life Series are to inform, educate, and enrich Christian persons and inspire them

    a. to become acquainted with the complex dynamics of marriage and family living;
    b. to pinpoint those attitudes, behavior skills, and processes which nurture health and wholeness in relationships rather than sickness and fragmentation;
    c. to consider marriage and family today in light of the Judeo-Christian faith.

As editors of the Judson Family Life Series, we are committed to making available the latest in family-life theory and research and to helping Christian families discover pathways to wholeness in relationships. Every attempt will be made by the authors to apply new insights to the realities of daily living in marriage and the family.

Other volumes in the series will focus on the stages of marriage, divorce and remarriage, parenting, and nurturing faith in families. Each will be designed to deal with specific issues in marriage and family living today.

As are many of the other authors in this series, Wallace Charles Smith is a trusted personal friend, known to us as Wally. He is also a respected faculty colleague. On occasion we have had the privilege of worshiping at Calvary Baptist Church in Chester, Pennsylvania, where Wally has been senior pastor for over a decade. Wally follows in the steps of his learned and prestigious pastoral mentor, J. Pius Barbour, who is an outstanding leader in the black community.

We have walked alongside Wally in a growth pilgrimage which has progressed and deepened with each year of study and experience. Wally began to focus on his deep concern for quality life in the black family while completing his thesis requirements for the doctor of ministry degree. As his mentors, we have watched that concern continue to expand and grow. The book you are about to read is his latest formulation.

In contrast with other books in this series which are written for couples or families, this volume is directed toward the black church and its ministry. You will discover the appropriateness of this focus as Wallace Smith discusses how the black church, in responding to a historical legacy marked by deep suffering, humiliation, and pain, formed a community of brothers and sisters in Christ who literally became an extended family. When needs are real and acknowledged, the church responds with care.

In some places in his book Dr. Smith writes as a *priestly* voice, lifting up the qualities of the black church which have brought healing, wholeness, and hope to the black people. He writes as a *pastoral* voice when he observes how our society continues to bring pain, hurt, and brokenness into the lives of its black citizens. He writes as a *prophetic* voice when he challenges the black church to respond with appropriate change to address the complex issues of our time. We have learned much through our dialogues with Wally.

Through Wally's voice via the written word, we invite you to enter into dialogue with this creative thinker and spokesperson for God. While the book is written primarily to the black church, through our own reading of the manuscript we ourselves have been led not only to expand and deepen our understanding of the ministry of the church in the life of black families but also to think through the nature and shape of the church's ministry in the life of all families. We consider Dr. Smith's volume to be a milestone contribution to the church and family ministry.

We are indeed joyous as we present to you *The Church in the Life of the Black Family,* by Wallace Charles Smith.

Jan and Myron Chartier
Eastern Baptist Theological Seminary
Philadelphia, Pennsylvania

Acknowledgments

M any persons have participated in the development of this book. Chief among them is my wife, Elaine, who provided a listening ear as this material was developing, and my seven-year-old daughter, Christen, who encouraged me simply by being herself.

I am indebted also to my parents, George and Zelma Smith, for all their unfailing support; my mother-in-law, Anne Wiggins; and father-in-law, Tom; my only brother by birth, George; his wife, Dottie, and son, Branch; also my brothers and sisters in the Spirit: Charles and Mary Jo Booth, Levi and Etta Baldwin, William J. Hand, and Jesse Wendell Mapson.

I also owe much thanks to our family of students, faculty, administrators, and staff at Eastern Baptist Theological Seminary. They provided an academic environment and much needed encouragement. Particular thanks must go to Myron and Jan Chartier. They are both mentors and friends. Thanks also to Marcia Patton, who put so much time into the technical areas and the editing, and to Danny Cortes for his untiring efforts.

The members of the Chester Community Improvement Project have also played an important part in the development of this book. Their assistance provided me a workshop in which to develop my family-centered theology. I am grateful to Salem Schuckman, Dana Lyons, Father John McFadden, Reverend James Jones, Matthew Jenkins, Wilson Harris, John Gibson,

Herman Dawson, Ed Collins, Frank Pierson, Janet Dickerson, Eugene Lang, and the many administrators, faculty, and students of Swarthmore College who supported our work.

Finally, to the Calvary Baptist Church of Chester I owe in some ways the greatest debt. They as a church "mentored" me. The theology that I never could have received in seminary I learned there. My appreciation of the church as extended family I received from them. For these reasons, I dedicate this book to the families in and the family of Calvary Baptist Church.

Contents

Introduction

This is a book on pastoral theology. It is also a book on family theology. It is designed as a resource for both pastors and lay leaders in churches that are working on ministries with families. This book is based on the generalization that the black church and the black family have the same roots and similar expressions. Dr. J. Deotis Roberts says in the summary of his book *Roots of a Black Future:*

> We have studied the history and sociology of the black family and have allowed our doctrine of the church in the black tradition to emerge out of the context. The extended family has been employed as a way of imaging the black church. Since our goal has been to make these two primary black institutions mutually supportive, it has been proper to use the family image in reference to a black ecclesiology. . . . Since black families are the source of the black church's life and growth, the measure of its ministry to black families will determine the quality of its own mission.[1]

These words act as a focal point for the purpose and direction of this book. In these pages we will attempt to establish what the black family has endured, the sources out of which it has been formed, and the directions that it and the church must take cooperatively if the awesome problems facing black America will ever be remedied.

As one who pastors, I have found that the grist out of which the thinking for this book emerged is more than just scholastics. I have watched families struggle with an assortment

13

of devastating problems. I have shared the pain of families in which members have been accused of or convicted of theft, drug addiction, prostitution, rape, and murder. I have been involved with homeless families who have been so desperate for a place to live that squatting in abandoned houses was their only recourse. I have witnessed elderly persons lose all sense of autonomy because of homelessness, illness, and loneliness. I have heard the cries of children, parents, and the elderly as they have faced conditions of hopelessness. Through it all I have witnessed a remarkable fact—for these persons the church has been the central authenticating reality in their lives. When the world has so often been willing to say only "no" to these people, the church has said "yes." For black people the church has been the one place where they have been able to experience unconditional positive regard.

One case in particular that comes to mind is Miss Elvia Smith. Miss Smith has never been married. In spite of this she has raised four sons. She rarely, if ever, received any support from their father. The boys have all grown to be respectable young men. Two of them have completed college, and the others are preparing for college. I asked her specifically what place the church had for her in her relationship with her children. Her response was that the church was family. Through these trying times she was rarely condemned by church members, although her first son was born in the fifties when people were not nearly as understanding about such matters as they are today. She also informed me that the men in the church acted as role models for her children. The former pastor, the senior deacons, and several trustees were not only persons that her children looked up to but also persons from whom they received significant nurture. The church was not able to help her financially, but what the church *did* give her in spiritual and family support was extremely valuable for the successful rearing of her children.

The experience of Elvia Smith is not unique. Black families around the country have turned to their churches as the source of hope and inspiration in times of family crisis.

Sadly, all churches have not been as understanding as Elvia's. There are many who remember vividly the horror stories of unwed mothers being driven from the churches by pastors, officers, and members who demanded public apologies for the mistakes that these young people made.

By and large, however, the dominant attitude of the churches toward family pain and suffering has been one of acceptance. It has always been a deeply felt sentiment among the majority of the black people in this country that we had to care for our own.

It is not accidental that families in the churches have not experienced many of the problems that have been faced by those who remain outside the church fellowship. Whether consciously or unconsciously, the preaching and singing about hope have provided a support system for church families in crisis. In the black community the church has always forced its members to look forward to a brighter day. Some have criticized the black church for becoming, in Marxian language, "the opiate of the people." Those who have made that assessment really have not understood the strength of the black church. Only because of the intentional reiteration of a profound eschatology has the black church been able to prevent an entire race of people from breaking under the yoke of relentless oppression.

This book's goal is to articulate a theology that will help churches, pastors, and leaders be better able to develop their already existing gifts.

The book is arranged around three themes. The first is an examination of the history and traditions of the black family. The second develops a black family hermeneutic. This hermeneutic provides a critical core out of which churches can do family enrichment without having to rest their programs upon the often racist assumptions of the social scientists. The third theme is a compilation of suggestions for enrichment programs and some suggested curriculum topics to aid pastors and leaders in the practical task of developing family ministries in their churches.

The theological assumptions of this book rest with the belief that God the Creator is also the parent of humankind. God is the one who indeed is, as we so often preach, mother to the motherless and father to the fatherless. God is a friend who sticks closer than a brother. As a parent, God is in relationship with us, not as some abstract absent premise but as a living, breathing, caring friend who is only a prayer away. Yet God is also Creator and because we are the creation, God and God alone knows how to fix us. Dr. Samuel Proctor, of the Abyssinian Baptist Church in New York, said in a sermon preached at Eastern Baptist Seminary in Philadelphia that he once had a foreign car that never ran properly until he finally had the good sense to take it back to the people who made it. Similarly, the social sciences provide rich insights, but psychology and sociology are human enterprises subject to the same weaknesses of all creation. Black folk have always known that God our Parent is ultimately also God our Creator and therefore the one to go back to when we have trouble "running properly."

As parent, God is both Father and Mother. Although masculine language is almost always used to describe God, black Christians have always been equally nurtured by the image of the mother eagle stirring its nest. Indeed, "The Eagle Stirreth Its Nest," after Martin Luther King, Jr.'s "I Have a Dream" speech, is probably the most famous sermon preached by a black in America. It was written by Dr. C. L. Franklin, who passed away in 1984. That sermon has been heard by hundreds of thousands of blacks throughout America through its distribution as a best-selling religious record.[2] Along with "Dry Bones" the "Mother Eagle" text has probably been one of the favorite sermon texts of churchgoing black persons for several centuries. I do not use this argument as definitive proof but only as an indication of the deep psychical feeling of black people that they have understood God to be both Father and Mother.

Scripture has been *the* authority in the lives of millions of black Americans. Debates about inerrancy have never really been critical to the black community. The experience of truth was enough for blacks to feel that God was doing the inspiring. There was, however, the wisdom within the black community to understand that certain statements were or were not worthy of God. Black preachers never saw inerrancy in "Slaves in all things obey your masters on earth" (Colossians 3:22) or in the curse of Ham (see Genesis 9:25). Some people have noted critically that black preachers opted for a canon within the canon. This observation is a valid criticism, but the fact remains that statements worthy of God were viewed as authoritative sources of truth. A statement was worthy of God if it spoke of freedom, equality, and justice. It was unworthy if it spoke of repression and injustice.

The measuring stick of the worthiness of a text was Jesus, our elder brother. Black Christology has always been done from below.[3] It focuses on Christ's historical personality, not the cosmic ramifications of his redemptive work. In many ways the Christology from below was quite different from that of the European rationalists, but the Christology from below group did share with the rationalists the sense that the incarnation was the critical starting point for the articulation of the faith. Because God was present in Jesus, the slave saw hope. Eschatology was grounded in the fact that the Baby in the manger with all his vulnerability was indeed the most powerful force to have ever lived. Through kinship with him, the powerless could sense a time when they would be empowered. Future hope, however, also had a present tense. The slaves came to see that in their ability to endure they were displaying a moral superiority which could only be possible if the God who was coming was already in their hearts.

The historicity of Jesus was carefully balanced for blacks through the experience of the Holy Spirit. The Third Person in the Trinity really is what has kept blacks from allowing their Christology from below to degenerate into dry rationalism. The brothers and sisters who gathered around the campfire may have been praying and singing about the "Sweet Little Jesus Boy" (a traditional Negro spiritual), but they were tarrying until the Holy Spirit came by. The experience of freedom could not happen until the Holy Spirit touched a person. When the Holy Spirit touched, the individual cried, danced, jumped, shouted, and most importantly was released momentarily from oppression. Through the experience of the Holy Spirit the individual and freedom became one. Even today a preacher or a choir that does not feel the Holy Spirit and does not help others to feel the presence is doomed to dwindling effectiveness. There is absolutely no question that the Holy Spirit is the *dunamis,* the "power of God" in action.

Just as the Trinity models the fact that God is in relationship with self, the church is a place of relationship. The church is family. Slavery did everything humanly and satanically possible to destroy the black family. The church kept the concept of family alive. God was the Parent, but those who gathered came together as a few of God's "helpless children." As God's children, blacks understood the nature of the church to be the performance of these rituals which cemented family members to each other and to God. The *diakonia* of the church, i.e., the "work of the church," was led in the Baptist churches by the deacons, who were the elder brothers. They assisted the pastor in making sure that when the body of Christ came together it was in the proper frame of mind for worship. Through prayers, singing, and testifying, the deacons set the stage for the pastor. Assisting the deacons was usually a mothers' board, a deaconess board, or an amen corner who also took responsibility in "getting the fire started" for the pastor. Both groups also kept order and saw to the proper care of whatever worship space was available. When the preacher "came on," it was his job to recreate new members ritualistically through baptism, to edify the body ceremonially through the serving of the Lord's Supper, and to admonish and exhort the body rigorously through the preaching of the Word.

The mission of the church was reaching out to those in need. Blacks have always been mission-minded. The black Baptist churches of America are still called missionary Baptist churches. It is through this strong sense of reaching out that black churches have historically touched black families. We will explore this further in the first chapter, but in its mission the black church often shared the same goals and delimitations of black families.

In its missionary outreach the black church modeled a concept of sufferers reaching out to fellow sufferers (a concept very consistent with a theology of the cross). Reaching out was inclusive. Slavery did not permit the luxury of male chauvinism. Men, women, and children suffered equally; so the church reached out comprehensively. Single mothers, orphans, widows, and widowers were all sought out to come as they were. The inclusiveness was possible because of the family paradigm. Evangelism in the black context was not just a church growth scheme; it was the adopting of someone from some other family into one's own family.

The consummation for black people will be the final overcoming. It will be at that time that the little Jesus boy of whom they have sung will return. The Holy Spirit's power that they felt when they shouted will have all creation shouting. The rocks of racist mentalities will be forced to repent and cry out. Mountains will be skipping like lambs. The glory of the Lord will be revealed. All flesh will see it together. The lions of licentious behavior will be forced to lie down with the lambs of light. The black church and the black family will see the fruition of their songs of faith:

"Great Day! Great Day, the righteous marching.
Great Day! God's going to build up Zion's walls.
This is the day of jubilee. God's going to build up Zion's walls!
The Lord has set His people free. God's going to build up Zion's walls!" [4]

1

The Black Church: Facing the Crisis of Family Living

In this chapter and in chapter 2, I will attempt to develop a clear picture of both the problems facing black families and the strengths of black families. A clear understanding of the issues is essential to the development of successful family ministries programs. Let me begin this chapter by articulating some of the critical issues through a series of questions.

First, is the black family a matriarchy?[1] Second, did slavery totally destroy black family structure?[2] Third, is black culture traceable through African retentions to customs and traditions of the motherland?[3] Fourth, does the black female have an identity independent of the stereotypes held of her by whites (male and female) and by black males?[4] These questions are certainly not exhaustive, but they do express some of the most widely debated issues facing the black family. These questions do not have easy answers. Both black and white scholars have been attempting to address these issues for years. The importance of raising such issues at the beginning of this work is twofold: One, these questions point to the confusing images that blacks have had foisted upon them by those who have examined the issue of family; two, the questions outline the important points which a theology based upon the paradigm of the black family must address.

Many studies have come out recently which have dealt with the rising trends of brokenness experienced by the black family. The problem with these studies is that they have not taken into account the critical importance of understanding the history and role of the church in its relationship to the black family.[5] The black family has its strengths and weaknesses, but there are strengths which often go overlooked by researchers. These undiscussed strengths are directly tied to the theology of the black church.

The black family's chief strength is its extended nature. More will be said about this later, but as an initial statement, it is important to point out that the two skills which have allowed for the survival of the black family, throughout the period of slavery and beyond, are its adaptability to change and its extended (rather than nuclear) structure.

To establish a black family theology, one must understand and appreciate these key family strengths. The knowledge of these important family attributes is crucial to the task because the black church is an extension of the black family. Some black liberation theologians, while claiming to be doing theology from below, have too often overlooked the family model as a way of describing the genius of the black church experience. Considering the enormity of white racism, which is the cause of the black family's problems,[6] the time has certainly come to reestablish the critical necessity of family and church cooperation.

Historically the church and family have provided that cooperation. Phenomenologically the black church in America developed out of the deprivation and oppression experienced by the slaves. In so doing, the black church existed as a support system for the oppressed at society's breakpoints. Without question the worst break point in this slavocracy was the separation of family members from one another. Mothers, fathers, sons, and daughters were consistently sold away at the masters' whims. The church evolved as a new family for those who were continually being uprooted from their original families.

Sadly for many blacks, the secularization of the twentieth century has exacted a great price. The church no longer occupies the central position of authority in the life of blacks that it once did. This fact has a great impact on the family. Families who are the most broken are families who also are at the lower end of the socioeconomic scale. Studies also indicate that it is primarily this group of the so-called underclass that is not being reached by churches.[7] Churches must develop ways to build bridges into this segment of the black community, or else the poverty-related problems faced by these people will continue to erode the family's effectiveness.

A way that these bridges might be built is through rethinking the very core of black theology. Black theologians have not by and large dealt with the potential good that might result if the black family was used as the model for church growth and development. Often black theologians discuss praxis as a starting point for doing theology, but what they ultimately wind up with is a theology based on the ideals which emerged from the Enlightenment. The genius of the black religious system is that it is alive. It is not a system that is a servant to print, media, or linear logic. This liveliness provides a genuine opportunity for the black church to base its theology on some novel premises. The model of the black extended family as a way of understanding the intricacies of the God-human encounter provides that unique premise.

The first task of theology is to develop a way of moving inside the theological circle. For Schleiermacher this was the "leap of faith." For Barth, it was the Word. For black theology, the model of the family can provide that entrance.

In an unpublished paper, Dr. Myron Chartier developed a theological primer based on the family model. He said,

> The Gospel has the power to liberate men and women from the contemporary forms of enslavement in a new community, the church. Central to Christian community is an intimate relationship with God through the empowering work of the Holy Spirit. This same spirit has led these believers into a reconciling interpersonal relationship with one another. Indeed, the Gospel of God binds men and women to one another as well as to God.[8]

He continued, "Although the Apostle Paul shows a strong preference for the body metaphor, its inadequacy with respect to organic unity leads him to employ the language of human relationships, especially family relationships." [9] Dr. Chartier's truly insightful piece examines the ways in which areas of health in family relationships are similar to the healthy signs witnessed in a church.

The black theologian, because of the extended nature of the black family, has a broader base to work from than does the white theologian who works from the nuclear model.

One purpose of this book is to establish the paradigm of the black extended family system as a praxis out of which theology can be exercised. A second purpose of this book is to present the potential for liberation available to blacks through a cooperative effort between churches and families. The assumptions critical to the realization of these goals are as follows:

(1) That the black family has shown marvelous survival and adaptive skills through extraordinary hardship;

(2) That African retentions and particularly the concept of extended family greatly aided in overcoming slavery's horrors;

(3) That white ideals of nuclear family structure and role need not necessarily be adhered to for a family to experience wholeness;

(4) That black women through the endurance of the double jeopardy of blackness and femaleness have been forced to develop a unique identity which has been largely misunderstood by white male theologians, feminists, and, sadly, many black male theologians as well.

C. Eric Lincoln has provided an inspiration for attempting unique ways to explore contextualization in black theology. He said,

> The Black church has traditionally relied upon a preached theology. . .Now that era may be past. The Blacks of this generation, and possibly for generations to come, are going to write their own theology in the light of their circumstances and needs.[10]

In the midst of the increasingly unacceptable realities of black unemployment and underemployment, the effects on the family have been devastating. Certainly no problem in black life needs any more serious attention. Public education is deteriorating. Crime has reached epidemic proportions. In the urban North some cities have an abandoned housing rate as high as one dwelling out of three. The ultimate absorber of all these problems is the family. With these problems it is not surprising that blacks in the seventies experienced the fastest rise, of any group, in the percentage of one-parent families. Studies consistently point out that the family will almost always reflect the problems of the society in which it exists. In 1981, 47.1 percent of black families with children were female-headed. Female-headed households are one large factor for the slow progress blacks have made in the last two decades to remove themselves from poverty level existence.[11]

Again, it is clear that the abhorrent conditions faced by blacks in America are continuing to draw the strength and life out of the black family. A cooperative effort between church and family to pool resources and reverse this trend is no longer a luxury. It is a necessity.

A Cooperative Strategy

When the black family has managed to survive in spite of societal exegencies, it has done so largely through the way in which it has drawn on the church for inspiration and for resources. The black church emerged as such a force in the life of blacks because it filled a real need. For the families that were being torn asunder by slavery, the black church became the place of nurturing and socialization. "Brother" or "sister" was not some abstract fundamentalism. It was a concrete way of expressing through the church the familial interrelatedness which, through the slave system, was often denied nuclear family members.[12]

The black family and the black church have drawn on each other for support and nurture. For them to develop a cooperative strategy suitable for dealing with the enormity of the problems, several shared realities must be understood. The first is that the black community is a suffering community. That the black family has experienced suffering is unquestionable. Those who have attempted to paint the black during slavery and through the Reconstruction as the "happy darky" have drawn the image more from wishful thinking than from reality. The black family experienced a depth of sin and pain at the hands of racism which can only be described as an experience of the Antichrist. That sense of suffering has been the ground out of which the black family and black church have developed. The black extended family lent to the church the model of social welfare and concern. This model created for the black church a paradigm in which the sharing of goods and resources for the care of the needy was accomplished. This attitude of the church produced involvement in education, in feeding the hungry, and in working with the homeless. Out of this extended family concept of a suffering community, the church evolved a dominant mind-set that the pastor (who functioned as chief of the tribe) was also responsible for the radical political action necessary to achieve for the church family the material necessities to deal with a racist world.

A secondary reality is that the black family shares with the black church the concept of inclusive community. A component of the western African family and religious system was a reverence for the aged and a unique and special space for women. The aged were the patriarchs and matriarchs. They were the ones soon to become the ancestors who in the spirit world demanded a certain amount of honor and respect. The American concept of placing elderly persons in separate care centers is an abomination to those of African descent. No matter how much bother or how troublesome, the aged were kept in the home out of reverence and respect. Women also had a special place in western African societies. To be sure, male dominance was the status quo, but to the Ashanti, a west African tribe from which many black Americans descended, the woman was the soul of the tribal structure. If men were the heads of society, then women in Ashanti culture certainly were the hearts. Some of this is still seen in the way in which black women by and large have not aligned themselves with the largely white feminist movement. In spite of the continued perpetuating of male/ female stereotypes within the black culture, black women have felt more in touch with the need for black people to be free than with the need for women internationally to unite. The feeling among many black women is that unless racism is totally eradicated, unification of women leaves black women washing the master's clothes and caring for the master's children—the new twist being that the master is now a white woman, not a white man.

The black family as an inclusive community was also an adoptionist community. In this context evangelism was done in the black church. The inclusion into membership was the saving of a sinner and also the grafting into the entire reality of that church a new family member who, in turn, became a full participant in the life and customs of that church. It is here that the black church as extended family obtains much of its identity. For black people a family member is not one who necessarily shares some blood kinship. He or she is one who has come to share joys, loves, pains, and struggles mutually.

The third reality that the black family has shared with the black church is the image of a hopeful community. As a hopeful community the black family has always modeled a practical eschatology. The spirituals and the sermons of the black church grew out of that mind-set. Black theology/sociology was a consistent belief that the better life, which was yet to come, was what gave one the ability to endure and in so doing made the unendurable bearable. Dr. David Shannon, former president of Virginia Union University, delivered a message at the Hampton Ministers' Conference in which this theme of the dual tracking of the spirituals was developed. He contended that the slave songs were consistent with the African world view of spirit and matter as being integrated. From this world view the slaves sang songs which were both codifications for events of physical liberation ("Roll Jordan Roll" was a coded message indicating a departure of the underground railroad) and an indication that the freedom train was not just "earthbound," but also heaven bound. The black church and family became the repositories of this hope. Through the extended family, blacks were able to insure that the powerful forces of slavery could never totally sever the ties to the African motherland and freedom.

The concept of the family as hopeful community was driven home in a class at Eastern Seminary on the black family. The discussion moved into the area of illegitimate births among teenagers and how many grandparents were becoming parents again by taking major responsibility in helping with the rearing of these grandchildren. A white woman in the class raised the issue of how despairing a situation this is. The black women in the class responded with a much different outlook. For each one her position was that "We don't have time to be despairing. Our grandchildren need to be celebrated as ours whether they are branded illegitimate or not." This celebration of life is basic to African people. The right-to-life groups do not cite the illegitimacy rate among black teenagers as one of the prime ex-

amples that blacks almost more than any other culture reverence life. Abortions by and large are not taken as a way out
for unwed mothers. This was true even before government cut-
backs on subsidized abortions.

The time has come for a reinterpretation of the black family
which gets beyond the overworked concepts of matriarchy or
brokenness versus strength. There is no question that the black
family was broken by slavery. The argument for the family's
strength, however, does not rest with the persons like Guttman
who want to interpret that strength from an assimilationist
perspective.[13] The strength of the black family must ultimately
be measured by its extraordinary contribution to black ecclesiology. In turn, that ecclesiology provides the potential for the
combined efforts of units of black extended families to step up
the movement towards liberation. Movement towards liberation is accomplished through the linkage of church and family.
It is accomplished by encouraging blacks to extend themselves
beyond brokenness for the purpose of finding family intimacy
within a church environment. In this church environment oppressed blacks will find others who share in the commonality
of oppression. As the nuclear family in all its brokenness comes
to the church, it finds a place where surrogate mothers and
fathers, brothers and sisters, uncles and aunts are willing to
receive them and adopt them into their fold. Single parents of
either sex may be afforded role models of the opposite sex to
whom children can relate. Youngsters who have known only
violence can receive love. Senior citizens who are talked about
by the majority culture as if they were faceless numbers can
have faces and voices. The black family has so influenced the
black church that it is indeed a home for the homeless when
maximizing its potential as the place where Jesus is.

2

What Is the Black Family?

If ministry to the black family is to be effective, it must be based upon adequate understanding. The purpose of this chapter is to explore the issues surrounding the question "What is the black family?" Because the uniqueness of the black family has rarely been given fair treatment by many researchers, we must begin by tracing its development historically.

The African Family Structure

It first must be stated that family stability is a trademark of the western African societies where most of the forebears of America's black population originated. However, the family structures of western Africa were not always of the Western European conjugal model. This model did exist, but the primary family model of western Africa was the consanguineal (blood-related) model.

> African families, like those in other parts of the world, embody two contrasting bases for membership: consanguinity, which refers to kinship that is commonly assumed or presumed to be biologically based and rooted in blood ties, and affinity which refers to kinship created by law and rooted "in law." Conjugality refers specifically to the affinal kinship created between spouses.[1]

[1]Niara Suderkasa, "Interpreting the Afro-American Heritage in the Afro-American Family Organization," p. 40 in *Black Families,* edited by Harriet McAdoo. Copyright © 1981 by Sage Publications, Inc. Reprinted by permission of Sage Publications, Inc.

The African family structure, unlike the European structure, tends to form around consanguineal cores of adult siblings. The groups that formed around these core members "included their spouses and children." [2] When African people were married, they "tended not to go off and form new nuclear groupings but instead joined an already existing compound of adjoining or contiguous dwellings" [3] composed of the extended family members.

In addition to the consanguineal structure in most African societies, there also existed a conjugal structure which was quite different from the European model and often polygynous in makeup. "A number of Western scholars have chosen to characterize the polygynous conjugal family as several distinct nuclear families with one husband/father in common." [4]

It must be stressed, however, that in the African family system it was the consanguineal rather than the conjugal model that was paramount. The consanguineal structure was the central factor in such critical family realities as decision making, settling internal disputes, and the inheritance of land titles, among others. These matters were settled not on the basis of spouse relationship but upon the blood ties of the family compound.

The structure then existed so that the eldest male was most often the head of the family compound. Along with the elders of the group, he was responsible for settling all internal (including conjugal) disputes. Decisions were made separately rather than jointly and husbands and wives often had very distinct responsibilities within the group.

"Excepting those areas where Islamic traditions overshadowed indigenous African traditions, women had a good deal of control over the fruits of their own labor." [5] An interesting result of this was that in spite of the rigidly paternalistic nature of the society, husbands had little control over their wives' properties. In fact, wives in these groupings had considerably more power and influence than did their European sisters.

The socialization of the young was a responsibility of the entire compound. Although the conjugal family had special duties, it was the consanguineal family which ultimately gave the child a sense of identity and self.

The stability of the family was not dependent upon the success of the individual conjugal units. In fact, divorce and re-marriage were rather easily accepted in the larger extended structure. Spouses were selected as lifetime compassionate and passionate lovers, but it was never expected that an individual was to be the one totally responsible for the spouse's every need for his or her entire life. The African family system was characterized by "respect, restraint, responsibility, and reciprocity." [6]

What one realizes in examining the African extended family structure is that the place of women was certainly much different from the Western world where polygynous structures were viewed as totally demeaning to women. The African structure was built on a mutual respect of women, men, and children. The uniqueness of this system can be seen in the way illegitimacy was handled. Women who had clandestine relationships with men other than their spouses reared offspring of these unions with the same care and love as children of the conjugal unit. The extended system prevented strongly violent reactions to such occurrences. Persons in the extended system were spared the jealousies which a purely nuclear structure fosters because partners did not see themselves as totally belonging to each other. All persons in this system belonged to the compound, not to any one individual.

Historically, one example of the African family system was found in the Ashanti. Their family system displayed a marvelous balance of respect, restraint, responsibility, and reciprocity. Fathers were responsible for the obedience and moral deference of their children, but with that strictness came tenderness also. An Ashanti proverb reads, "A man has no hold over his children except through their love." Mothers were given reverential treatment but they also functioned in very practical ways. In spite of our western Freudian hang-ups, an Ashanti mother was to be her son's best friend. She was his chief consul in all matters, be they practical, emotional, or psychical. The Ashanti mother also was responsible for seeing that her daughters grew up in daily and unbroken intimacy with her. The daughters learned from the mothers all the feminine skills and traits of character.

Slavery and the Black Family

Whatever the relative strengths or weaknesses of the African family structure, it must be remembered that African peoples were also forced to face the holocaust of slavery. Slavery systematically attempted to destroy the black family. The insidiousness of its evil cannot be minimized.

Throughout the sunless experience of slavery, families were yanked from the motherland and brought as strangers to this alien place. As C. Eric Lincoln poetically stated, "Slavery was a man getting up for a breath of fresh air and winding up on a boat destined for a new world." [7]

Once Africans arrived in the New World, every attempt was made to strip them of name, dignity, and culture. Even more tragic, morals were forcibly stripped away was well. Black males were encouraged to be irresponsible breeders who served nothing more than two functions—mating and manual labor. Black females were accosted by masters who forced them to have sex and bear unwanted children. To make this systematic rape of black women even worse, laws were changed so that the inheritance for all these mulatto children would be traced through the woman's lineage, cutting these children off from access to the master's capital.

Because of the way racism enforced its power through economics, sex amongst the slaves was viewed by the master as a matter of dollars and cents. The encouraging of casual breeding amongst slaves and the wanton rape of slave women were the fastest ways to increase the birth rate and improve capital gain. In the words of Robert C. Williamson, "It is difficult to overestimate the dismal effects of slavery on family life." [8] He further states, "Because of the slave owner's encouragement of high birth rate as a means of increasing wealth, little consideration was given to the establishment of a firm marriage bond. Occasionally, the offspring of mixed liasons were given freedom. It is estimated that one-third of the half million free Negroes in 1860 were mulattoes." [9] It can never be stressed enough that the huge mulatto population in America is the result of the rape of black women by white masters.

Slavery enforced the equality of black males and females through equal pain. The master never treated the slave women with any of the daintiness with which he treated white women. Slave women were forced to work in the field side by side with males. They were punished with equal severity and the physical realities of pregnancy and pre- or postnatal care were never considered as reasons for time out from work.

After emancipation the situation for the family did not improve. The ineffectiveness of the Freedman's Bureau insured that the problems begun during slavery would never adequately be dealt with. Again, economics exacerbated the problem.

The demise of the agrarian life in the South struck a particularly vicious blow to black males, who were trained only in farming. Work was scarce to nonexistent. What little work was available was the demeaning and menial labor reserved for maids. Although these positions were hellish nightmares of inadequate pay, overwork, and frequent rape by the employer, they were the only jobs black women could obtain. Again, racism and economics saw to it that through the unemployment of the male and the dehumanizing employment offered females, the black family suffered. During this period, the desertion rate for black males escalated. Much of what is said about the matriarchal structure of the black family began with observations that were made during this time.

When the western African concept of respect for women is coupled with the way women were forced into positions of equal suffering during slavery, the matriarchial argument takes on a new light. The severe economic pressures of post-Reconstruction America forced blacks to adopt whatever ways were necessary to survive. "Adapt" was what blacks did to survive slavery. It was also the way after emancipation that blacks handled their plight. As demeaning as it was, if the only work available was for women to clean the master's home, it was better to do this and survive than to allow racism to destroy the family totally.

As it is discussed by white sociologists, matriarchy is a myth. The myth is not that female-centered homes exist. The myth is that these female-centered homes point to male weakness. Weakness is not a word that can be used to describe either black males or females when one considers the awesome burdens that have been overcome by blacks since slavery. The only thing that the female-centered home indicates is that in the face of extraordinary pressure, the black family has somehow found the strength to survive. Jean Noble, writing in the *World Encyclopedia of Black People,* sees in all this what she calls the "myth of matriarchy":

> Societal oppression based on institutionalized efforts to keep black men subservient and dependent deprived black men of the expected role of sole bread winner in their families. Myths that their mothers, sisters, and wives were castrating black matriarchs simply because they were allowed to work aggravated black men's feelings of inadequacy. The fact that black women were only allowed to work at jobs white men did not want white women to undertake became forgotten in history as the avalanche of epithets and myths came forth to persuade everyone that black women were less desirable than white women. Spokeswomen for the women's liberation movement have commended the black woman's triumph over adversity. This attention is a small comfort to black women, however, because it is the respect and love of black men, and a yearning to create a partnership with them, that is paramount in black women's lives.[10]

The Roots of the Matriarchal Controversy

In establishing a historical overview it is important to understand the technical dimensions of the descriptions made of the black family. The first point that must be made is that there have been contrasting approaches to the study of black families historically. The first major school is the pathological dysfunctional school, which holds the assumption that the black family is "unstable, disorganized, and unable to provide its members with the social and psychological support and development needed to assimilate fully in American society." [11] The second is the cultural relativity school which assumes that black American culture possesses an integrity that has origins in the African cultural heritage which focuses on the strengths rather than the weaknesses of the black family.

Both schools do hold that black and white families are different. Where they go their separate ways is in assessing the roots of these differences. The pathological dysfunctional school had as its leading exponent E. Franklin Frazier. Frazier's major concern was twofold: "Refute the argument advanced by Melville Herskovits that much of black life is a continuation of

[11]Jualynne Dodson, "Conceptualizations of Black Families," p. 24 in *Black Families,* edited by Harriet McAdoo. Copyright © 1981 by Sage Publications, Inc. Reprinted by permission of Sage Publications, Inc.

African cultural forms and empirically demonstrate Robert E. Parks's race relations cycle." [12] Frazier rejected the notion that indiscriminate sex or extramarital sex among blacks was a carryover from Africa. He felt that such examples of promiscuity must be a result of the effects of slavery.

The most infamous result of the thinking of this pathological dysfunctional school came in 1965 when the Office of Policy Planning and Research of the United Stated Department of Labor under the leadership of Patrick Moynihan developed a document entitled *The Negro Family—The Case for National Action.* "This report repeatedly cited Frazier as support for its conclusions that the black community was characterized by broken families, illegitimacy, matriarchy, economic dependency, failure to pass armed forces entrance tests, delinquency and crime." [13]

Moynihan's thesis further stated that the "matrifocal" family is largely a factor in the poor progress of blacks in America. His thesis has received a great deal of criticism, largely from black sociologists. A case could be made that concepts such as Moynihan's lie at the root of the identity problems experienced by black people, but rather than make that case, let us look at problems with the Moynihan document.

The first problem with accepting the Moynihan thesis is the realization that it was the observation by a white man of a culture that in some ways was totally alien to him. The sad reality is that much of what has been said about the black family and black folk generally both in slavery and in freedom has been based on the observations of whites.

J. Deotis Roberts cites an example of this type of thinking in a speech given by President Lyndon Johnson at Howard University in 1965. Johnson's speech, in capsulized form, articulated several white observations of the black family. He supported a nuclear family structure as the ideal family model; he attacked the matrifocal structure of the black family as being a source of the family's weakness; he cited oppression of black males as the central cause of black family breakdowns.[14]

Although Johnson's speech delineated the basic assumptions of white sociologists, it must be noted that, E. Franklin Frazier notwithstanding, many black scholars have generally rejected these suppositions. They have raised their voices in dissent against the Western system of social evil which forced slavery upon the black race and then had the audacity to use purely white criteria to assess the black family's weaknesses.

It was that protest of black scholars and the pathological dysfunctional school which gave birth to the cultural relativity school. This school goes back to the Herskovits contention that African carryovers do exist in Western black cultures and that these heritages, once they are traced and understood, provide the key to understanding the black family.[15] "The cultural relativity view, primarily in reaction to the cultural ethnocentric [pathological dysfunctional] view, advocates that the black family is a functional entity. This conceptualization is largely advanced by Andrew Billingsley (1968), Virginia Young (1970), Robert Hill (1972), Wade Nobles (1974), and others."[16] This school of thought has drawn very heavily on the phenomena of African retentions and particularly on the concept of the African extended family as the dominant model of the black family system in America.

Colin Turnbull sums it succinctly, "The slaves who were exported to the Americas were Africans before they were slaves and Africans afterwards, and their descendants are still Africans today."[17]

Sociology and the Family

Black Americans then must not only ask, "What am I about?" but they must also ask, "What ought the family to be about?" if the question of survival is to be answered. In an essay, Suzanne Keller analyzes a debate on the family that took place between Malinowski and Briffault. She saw the difference in their opinions as resting on different definitions of the phenomenon "family."

> Malinowski defined the family as a legal union of one man and one woman with their offspring, bound by reciprocal rights and duties, cooperating for the sake of economic and moral survival. Briffault defined the family more and more broadly, as any association involving economic production and sexual procreation.[18]

Keller's quote states two opinions on the formula of family. When one deals with the question of the black family, these formulas ultimately lead to the question of matriarchy. The

Moynihan report of 1965 helped to fuel that fire:

> In effect, the Moynihan Report contended that low-income, urban
> Negro families were so unstable that equal opportunity legislation
> could do little to free them from "the cycle of poverty and disad-
> vantage". . .In support of his position, Moynihan cited statistics from
> the early 1960s to the effect that, compared with white families,
> Negro families were more likely to be dependent on welfare assis-
> tance, to have women with absentee husbands, daughters who bear
> illegitimate children, and high rates of crime.[19]

Charles V. Willie in his article "Intergenerational Poverty" [20]
answers the assertions made by Patrick Moynihan in his report
on the Negro family. Willie states that Moynihan's contention
(that a national effort to solve the problems of Negro Americans
and their family life is necessary) is based on inadequate assumptions. Moynihan viewed the weakness of the family structure as the principle source of most antisocial behavior in the
black community. He concludes that this "tangle of pathology"
is capable of perpetuating itself. The fallacy of this, says Willie,
is in the assumption that values of blacks differ from values
of other ethnic groups. To assume that, and to assume that this
particular pathology is intergenerationally transmitted, is to
assume that poverty exists only because of internal factors. To
understand the black plight in America is first to be aware
that internal and external factors are so interrelated that where
one ends and another begins is never clearly defined.

The Malinowski-Briffault debate does seem to raise a crucial
question, for the family in general as well as for black families.
Can one talk about the weaknesses or strengths of the family
structure unless the phenomenon of family in general is basically understood and its definitions agreed upon? Contemporary black sociologists, such as Willie, are saying that because of the uniqueness of the black struggle, questions about
poverty and delinquency cannot be explained simply; a family
will respond to the aberrant conditions to which it must relate.
Talcott Parsons, in his article "The Normal American Family"
gives the following standard formula for family:

> It can then be said that, in a sense that has probably never existed
> before, in a society that in most respects has undergone a process
> of very extensive structural differentiation, there has emerged a
> remarkably uniform, basic type of family. It is uniform in its kinship

and household composition in the sense of confinement of its composition to members of the nuclear family, which is effective at any
given stage of the family cycle, and in its outside activities of its
members, e.g., jobs for adult men, some participation in the labor
force for women, school for children, and various other types of
community participation.[21]

This kind of statement from a scholar of Parsons's magnitude
constitutes a part of the confusing problem that the black family faces. Conformity to an ideal defined by the middle-class
majority of America is the definition of excellence or brokenness. However, in an article entitled "The Absent Father in
Negro Families: Cause or Symptom" [22] Wasserman found, in a
study of the school performance of children of lower-class black
families living in a low-income housing development, that there
is really no external criterion for evaluating the characteristics
of family life and how well it fosters educational achievement.
Indeed, the scores of some of the children from one-parent families were higher on scholastic and behavioral achievements
than the scores of children from two-parent families.

One reason given for the stress placed upon the superiority
of the two-parent nuclear family structure over any extended
family models is that most Western scholars build their designs
on heavily conservative, conventional models.[23] While these
scholars seem radical in their attempts to explain and understand exotic cultures, there is the very conservative thrust to
justify existing institutions and practices. The dominant model
of the family as it emerges in the writings of social scientists
is as follows:

1. The nuclear family—a man, a woman, and their children—is universally found in every human society, past
   and present.
2. The nuclear family is the building block of society. Larger
   groupings—the extended family, the clan, the society—
   are combinations of nuclear families.
3. The nuclear family is based on a clear-cut, biologically
   structured division of labor between man and woman,
   with the man playing the instrumental role of breadwin-
   ner, provider, and protector, and the woman playing the
   expressive role of housekeeper and emotional mainstay.
4. A major function of the family is to socialize children; that

is, to tame their impulses and instill values, skills, and
desires necessary to run the society.

5. Unusual family structures, such as mother and children
   or the experimental commune, are regarded as deviant
   by the participants as well as the rest of society and are
   fundamentally unstable and unworkable.[24]

I concede that this kind of thinking is basically enunciated
in the anthropological works of Westermarck, Lowie, and Malinowski. The impact of such thinkers on the overall social science concept of the family, however, is a strong one. To hold
these views is to relegate anything outside this norm to the
classification of deviance. Yet the pressures on these abnormal
families drastically cloud the picture so that their viability is
hard to ascertain. E. E. LeMasters estimates that one in ten
families in America is headed by a woman; yet these same
households constitute twenty-five percent of the so-called poverty groups in America.[25] (Of course, this figure raises the whole
question of women's comparative incomes in our society).
LeMasters's figures are not just for blacks, but for all families
in our society, and it must be stated that the pressures of pov-
erty-level living do seriously affect such things as higher educational pursuits. When describing the black perspective of
all this, Warren D. Tenhouten states in "The Black Family:
Myth and Reality" [26] that this assumed deviance was articulated essentially by Frazier, who describes four kinds of black
families: the martriarchal; the family akin to the traditional
white family with the father having undisputed authority; an
essentially patriarchal type originating in mixed black, white,
and Indian communities; and those of mixed ancestry who define themselves as a separated, isolated race, but were also
basically patriarchal. During the great migration of blacks from
the rural South to the urban North, matriarchal families were
basically unable to deal with the problems of an urban environment and resorted to charity for existence. Children ran
amuck, gangs were formed, and daughters were given to a high
level of illegitimate pregnancies.

Tenhouten takes exception with this thesis as being normative and also takes exception with the Moynihan report,
which he considers faulty in its methodology (which assumes
matriarchal dominance and male subservience). Some impor-

tant points which he believes Moynihan overlooks include the
following:

> One reason why black women (both poor and non-poor) are more
> apt to head families is a differential access to adoption. Most white
> women that have illegitimate babies are able to have them adopted.
> But since the demand for black babies is low, black women have
> comparatively limited opportunities to have their illegitimate chil-
> dren adopted and thus are more apt to keep them.[27]

Secondly, he says that the Moynihan thesis implies that black
men are emasculated and subdominant in their homes. "There
is, however, no empirical evidence showing that black men who
leave their wives do so because they are unable to play a dominant role in the family." [28] In addition, Tenhouten continues
to say that there are no statistics available concerning the sixty
percent of black homes with a husband present, which would
indicate that these husbands are emasculated and subdominant in comparison to their white counterparts.

Implications

It is clear that there are very conservative forces within the
social sciences which define the family from a very narrow
perspective. Working from a post-Enlightenment mind-set, these
scholars are developing an image of humankind which is largely rational and individualistic. Even when the term "family"
is used, it is really only used as an expanded description of the
individual. The problem with definitions such as these is that
they are not in keeping with the way family and relationships
and individuality are defined by many non-Western cultures.

The African concept of extended family is fundamentally
different from the European concept. It is based on the consanguineal rather than the conjugal unit. For this reason black
churches which are doing family enrichment must begin their
work with an almost total rejection of substantive amounts of
available material produced by white social scientists and theologians. Family enrichment programs for blacks can be successful only if there is a basic appreciation for the subtle yet
profound differences which go into the very process of defining
family.

Given the American context, there is no question that one
goal of a black family enrichment program must be to shore

up the strength of the nuclear family. On the other hand, the nuclear family must also be seen as fully in community with and linked with others. The results of this linkage with others can be defined as extended family if those others in the relationship share blood, or metaphorically, are linked through their shared pain, shared history, and shared hope of liberation. The black extended family is not just a gathering of nuclear families. It is a system which functions as more than the sum of its parts.

At this level the black church has always served as an extended family. It has been to varying degrees a contemporary expression of the African consanguineal model. Within the church structure there are found both stable nuclear families and a variety of differing family models. The variances may range from one-parent families in a nuclear arrangement to grandparents, uncles, aunts, or godparents serving as the primary parents for youngsters born outside the nuclear grouping.

What must be remembered is that a black family enrichment program in black churches will certainly want to work toward stable nuclear arrangements as a goal for black people. This is because the culture in which we find ourselves does not have the support systems for anything much beyond a conjugal model, and with the givens of our Western capitalist structure young blacks will be better able to advance economically and socially if the two-parent approach is adopted. Single parents in this culture have a difficult time making it economically. Beyond that fact, however, both biblically and theologically the two-parent model also lies at the heart of our Judeo-Christian faith. From a faith standpoint, this one fact alone means that strengthening two-parent families must be the church's goal.

On the heels of the previous statement, it must also be added that for black people a family enrichment program must not stop with the nuclear family. The nuclear family must always be seen as only a part (although an important part) of the extended family structure. All programs of family enrichment for the black church must be two-pronged. They must deal with helping to stabilize two-parent families, and they must also deal with helping to enhance the extended family support network and firming up the church's ability to develop personhood and positive self-image for those trapped outside the Western

accepted model of family. Women and men in one-parent relationships must be loved and nurtured. Persons living together outside of marriage must be counseled lovingly. Young people experimenting with premarital sex must be helped to respect and love themselves and their church so that they feel a
kinship and affinity which will allow them the strength to avoid
detrimental relationships. The elderly must be viewed as integral and functional church family members—not useless ap-
pendages. In the best concept of Paul's thoughts in Ephesians
5, mutual submission must be the guideline for effective black
family enrichment programs.

3

Personhood—
Being Made in
the Image of God

The social science debates over the structure of the family
show very clearly that in these discussions little or no
reverencing of African history and customs is put forth. Blacks
are an invisible people whom Europeans tried either to ignore
or to fit into their preconceived notions of right and wrong. The
result of all this for black people is a total denial of personhood.
Black people are raised in the West to be disrespectful of their
heritage and to hate themselves for the way they look, act, and
feel. A black family theology must begin its work by dealing
with the ugly scar that racism has placed upon the black psyche. This nasty scar has formed at the place where racism made
its first incision—the image of the self.

The Question of Self-Image

In his book *Prophesy Deliverance!* Cornell West raises the
question of black self-image as a pivotal problem in the arena
of the black plight in America. He says, "The basic challenges
presently confronting Afro-Americans are self-image and self-
determination."[1]

In discussing the genealogy of modern racism West points
back to the classical revival initiated in the early Renaissance
period (1200-1500) which reached its height during the high
Renaissance (1500-1530). He says, "The classical revival is important because it infuses Greek ocular metaphors and classical
ideals of beauty, proportion and moderation into the beginnings
of modern discourse."[2]

The classical revival was an attempt to return to the Greek notions of beauty and proportion which characterized this period. The most famous writer during this time was J. J. Winckelman. His book *History of Ancient Art* painted images of ancient Greece as a place of beautiful bodies. He laid down rules in art and aesthetics that should govern the size of eyes and eyebrows, of collarbones, hands, feet and especially noses. . . . Although Winckelman was murdered in middle life, never set foot in Greece, and saw almost no original Greek art (only one exhibition of Greek art in Munich), he viewed Greek beauty and culture as the ideal or standard against which to measure other people's cultures.[3]

The significance of this return to classical Greek standards is that it began flourishing about the same time that the scientific method began taking hold. The sciences became the validations by which these artistic notions were ground into the psyche of Western culture. "The genealogy of racism in the modern West is inseparable from the appearance of the classificatory category of race in natural history."[4]

Carolus Linnaeus, who wrote *Natural System* in 1735, and Georges Louis Leclerc de Buffon, who wrote *Natural History of Man* in 1778, were both scientists who developed systems of racial classification which either overtly or through implication suggested that African ancestry was inferior.

Johann Friedrich Blumenbach and Peter Camper, the first a founder of modern anthropology and the latter an anatomist, both used quasi-science as a way of establishing European facial characteristics as the ideals for all humanity. Peter Camper even went as far as to claim that facial angle (with respect to the slope of the face from the forehead to the chin) was an indication of ideal humanity. The perfect facial angle was 100 degrees which was achieved only by ancient Greeks. European facial angle was about 97 degrees, black people somewhere between 60 and 70 degrees.[5]

The anti-African sentiment became so strongly imbedded into the lives of Europeans that appalling racist slurs were delivered by such major Enlightenment thinkers as Jefferson, Kant, and Hume. For example, Hume said of blacks:

> I am apt to suspect the negroes, and in general all the other species of men (for there are four or five different kinds) to be naturally inferior to the whites. There never was a civilized nation of any other complexion than white, nor even any individual eminent either in action or speculation. No ingenious manufacturers amongst them,

no arts, no sciences. . . .
    In Jamaica they talk of one negro as a man of arts and learnings but tis likely he is admired for slender accomplishments, like a parrot who speaks a few words plainly.[6]

For those of us who grew up black in this country these statements strike a painful chord. They recall the days of skin lighteners, of hair straighteners, of wishing that our skin was not so dark or our lips not so thick. Many bright students developed poor study habits or began to feel that ultimately they could not compete with their white counterparts because they felt that being black meant they were inferior.

These things were not taught explicitly in the sixties, but they were attitudes that seeped through at every crack. Even television with its lily-white shows of the fifties and sixties gave a subtle message. The message was always somehow learned either subtly or through some overt encounter with racism: "If you are black, you are ignorant, dumb, lazy, or worthless."

Many in my high school class recall a white guidance counselor who invariably either attempted to steer black students into a vocational program or, if they were in college preparatory classes, to persuade them to attend black colleges. The underlying sentiment was that average blacks did not stand a chance in higher education, and brighter blacks did not stand a chance at white schools.

The problem of self-image among blacks is certainly clear. To be black means that for over six centuries European culture has with regularity been developing strategies to devalue black personhood. It is impossible to get a handle on the problems of crime, drug abuse, alcoholism, and rape unless one attempts to feel what it must be like for persons who do not have the extraordinary ego strength to overcome negative imaging. Even the so-called middle-class black bourgeoisie are affected by the same lingering negativity. They may not be as susceptible to crime as the so-called underclass, but often their societies are but pale, hollow reflections of white middle-class values. Many so-called underclass persons feel that even if their lives are fraught with violence and economic plight, they at least have not capitulated to the mind-rape that has caused so many upwardly mobile blacks to lose their identity and their souls.

It must be pointed out that the material cited as the historical source of the negative stereotypes of blacks comes from the disciplines of the social sciences. For this reason blacks must not look to the sciences for the correction of the problem. The debates of Moynihan, Frazier, and others just reaffirm the bankruptcy of the sciences when dealing with moral issues. The correction of the black self-image can only be achieved through a reestablishing of the theological principles out of which all humanity is ultimately defined.

God and Human Creativeness

A theology that takes its confessing out of the history and traditions of the church does well to begin its task with the concept of human createdness. The foisting upon any one group of a negative self-image is only possible if that group is some-how denied an understanding of having been created in God's image. The story of how humankind came to bear God's image is foundational to the entire process of authentic freedom. Oppression in any form, be it of male over female or white over black, can only exist if the oppressing group, through the power of their superior technology or through custom and tradition, refuses to see the oppressed as sharing the same degree of God's image as they.

Karl Barth discusses the concepts of fellowship and freedom as a key grounding in any theological anthropology. He says that humankind is ordained by God to be "in covenant relation" [7] with God and that this relationship with God is how human-kind determines the character of relationship with the other. Barth believes that the special mode of being for humankind is, in essence, a "being in fellow humanity." [8]

God then acts as the one who by the nature of our creation directs us into this concept of human mutuality. As persons, our being "fulfills itself in the encounter." This idea of fellow humanity is summed up by Barth when he says,

> God commands us to be what we are but this means that He takes man so seriously in his vocation to be in covenant with Him that He calls him to freedom in fellowship, i.e., to freedom with others. He calls him and finds himself by affirming the other, to know joy by comforting the other, and self-expression by honoring the other. [9]

Through this concept of the other or the neighbor, Barth sets down a very important point of departure for an understanding of the human family, of theological anthropology, and ulti-mately the God-human relationship. This concept is that all humankind is by creation in relationship and directed toward loving and appreciating one another. When this is held up as a standard, the negative imaging that the dominant culture has placed upon minority peoples is not only impossible to support philosophically, but it is also demonic.

For black people, using this biblical imagery as a starting point for developing a theology of the family is of the utmost importance because much of the confusion which comes about in assessing the black family's strengths and weaknesses comes about because those doing the defining have been working from a social science base.

Regardless of the work of Frazier, Moynihan, or Herskovits, the province of defining the black family in America must begin with the confession of faith. African retentions are helpful in defining the nuances of the reality, and the pathological dysfunctional school of thought helps one appreciate the depth of the problem. For the black American, however, either pole is the wrong starting point in the search for solutions. Black Americans have, since slavery, drawn their strength from the treasure house of the biblical story. It can only be in that same storehouse that the black American must now return if the awesome weight of racism and oppression is to be lifted. The Bible must be the starting point for this renewal of human community because it—not the social sciences—provides a revelation of the potential for transformation. The Bible also acts as humankind's touchstone of shared imagery. Holding biblical revelation as the authentic definer of human community is critical in a world where cultural and racial differences deny the possibility of any authentic dialogue. Through the revelation of God, language barriers, cultural subtleties, and sexual differences are all reduced from ultimate to penultimate concerns.

With biblical revelation as the starting point, it is important for a theology of the black family to take up the question of self-image and examine what in that revelation provides a story which has the potential to unravel the negative stories that blacks have been forced to bear for centuries.

Biblical Anthropology and Black Self-Image

The Bible has been the central source of authority for millions of black Americans. The Bible has been the precious story of God linked by the slaves in the canebrake and the cotton fields with African stories of overcoming.

The Bible has been understood by black folk to be a record of freedom. Scraps of its stories as overheard by the slaves became the foundation of a unique theology of liberation as embodied in the spirituals.

Unfortunately, however, the Bible was also taught by unscrupulous slavemasters as the authoritative source for obedience to one's master and acceptance of one's curse, which was marked by one's blackness.

For the black church to model the freeing power which is necessary to liberate persons from the negative myths that have been perpetrated upon its people, the Bible must be allowed to speak for itself and eisegesis such as that which produces the ludicrous interpretations of Ham's curse must be vehemently denied and replaced by a hermeneutic which lets God speak.

The concepts of self and self-image are addressed clearly and authoritatively in Genesis 1:26-27 by the concept of the *Imago Dei*[10] (*Image of God*). In that passage the generic and individual uniqueness of humankind is communicated clearly and precisely. Humankind is made "in the image of God." The image is both *selem* and *demuth*, i.e., it is both image and likeness expressed collectively; but it is also image expressed through individuality. In the uniqueness of createdness, human beings are appointed simply to be persons or to be selves. We are not God (our strivings to be God are the basis of our fallenness), but we are like God. We share with God an image and a "like-Godness," but our office is to be human and to exercise that created office by having dominion, or responsibility, over God's creation. Interrelational difficulties come when the paradox of createdness is not grasped. This paradox is simply that we find ourselves a part of the very creation over which we are instructed to have dominion. Problems between persons come when the responsibility aspect of dominion (God instructed us to do) is not extended to the most basic ecological perspective: the human duty to nurture and preserve relationships.

It is in the notion of the ecological responsibility of interdependent selves that blacks can find a note of hope. This hope can transform negative imagery by establishing a universal self-image not based on stereotypical models but based on the very stuff and substance of godly creativity. This model of universality has the potential to transcend the questions of male/female dominance and subservience and deal with the issue of human mutuality.

All persons can, if they so choose, trace the excellency of their being back to the stunning and unique act of creation in

Genesis 1:26-27, "and so God made humankind in his own image and in his own likeness" (paraphrased).

Black family members can find in the concept of *Imago Dei* the purest and most ancient Judeo-Christian notion of self-image. The potential of this relationship is that in spite of the deprivations of racism God's image within blacks has never been tarnished.

The author's feeling about Genesis 1:26-27 and its particular importance for self-image is based on the universal principles of human wholeness from which this text speaks. It is creation material and therefore quite ancient. It speaks of *adham*, mankind, as that which was created by God, i.e., not "white man" or "red man" but just "man"; and it also develops an idea which is critical to this book, namely, that humankind made in the image of God is made male and female.

It is by the role stereotyping of black males and black females that racists have since the times of slavery foisted onto blacks the images of "dominant female" and "irresponsible male." Genesis 1:26-27 by its very premise rejects either matriarchy or patriarchy as ideals and develops the concept that maleness and femaleness are coequal in participation in the *Imago Dei*.[11]

The Theological Significance of the *Imago Dei*

There are several concepts within the history of the interpretation of Genesis 1:26-27 that have been lifted up during various periods. The phrase "let us" was often thought to refer to God in consultation with other selves. Some early trinitarians made much of this concept. The concepts of image and likeness were often viewed as reference to body and spirit, and *adham* was viewed to be a proper name other than the generic, encompassing within the image of createdness the totality of maleness and femaleness.[12] These last two issues have profound implications for the way in which education to unravel the negative weave of racist stereotypes is done.

> Today more than any time, the question "What is Man?" is at the center of theological and philosophical concern. The number of studies that have taken this problem as their theme is almost innumerable. And yet, the fact that this problem has forced itself to the attention of contemporary thought does not take away a rather puzzling aspect of the problem itself; namely why should this be a problem? It would seem that there is nothing so widely and generally "known" in everyday experience as is man. It is not a problem of the "nature [of man]."[13]

What can be stated about humanity from the findings of this examination thus far is that *adham* is used in the text as the generic and should not be taken to mean a proper name.[14] This understanding of a man created as an archetype of humanity, with the two concepts being interchangeable, seems to be unique to the Hebrews (of the ancient Near Eastern peoples). This generic uniqueness consistently follows through historically. This fact is true for Septuagintal translation, Alexandrian interpretation, Patristic interpretation, and others. Second to the generic nature of creation is the fact that she/he also was created with consciousness. In the words of Sartre, humanity has both a reflective and pre-reflective cognito.[15] Humanity is separated from the animal kingdom because humanity is the only being (so far established) who is able to reflect on himself/ herself reflecting.[16] While developing a notion of humanity as "aspective yet holistic," [17] Frank Stagg says this about biblical interpretations of the concept of "self":

> Many terms are used in Scripture to stress the aspective nature of man, as seen from various perspectives. These terms are not employed consistently. A term may vary in meaning from passage to passage by the same author. Only context can disclose its intention in any given usage. Any of the terms may be used for the whole man, seen from a given perspective.[18]

These concepts are, according to Stagg, the following: *psyche,* which tends to be used for "soul," "life," "heart," or "self"; *soma,* denoting "body"; *sarx,* meaning "flesh"; and *pneuma,* meaning "body-spirit," "flesh-spirit," or "body-soul-spirit."

The main point about these words as they are used scripturally is that they are used holistically. Stagg develops this notion with his concept of the larger "house." [19] His contention is that

> Recovery of the biblical understanding of man as aspective but holistic opens the way to a richer understanding of salvation, a heavier responsibility in ministry to man, and even a more responsible care for God's good earth, the larger "body" or house ("ecology" is from *oikos,* "house") in which we live.[20]

He goes on to say that the biblical understanding of humanity allows for no dichotomy of matter and spirit. Those concepts are concepts that seeped into biblical faith through Orphic and Platonic corruptions. These notions are both non-biblical and ecologically fatal because they teach humanity to abhor rather than rejoice in that which God has created.[21] What then are

we to make of this self which is human? We must assert un-
equivocally that this self is a self only in relationship to other
selves. Genesis 1:27 (KJV) states this forcefully, "in the image
of God created he them." Had "in the image of God created he
him," been a repeat of the same singular pronoun there might
have been cause to see "self" or "psyche" as a singular entity
in and of itself; but the "them" as part of a follow-up clause in
opposition to male and female implies a relationship; and because of that relationship interrelatedness is integral to being.

Theological anthropology must necessarily see another dimension to the relationship of self to selves and that is in the
relationship of self to God. In the *Institutes* Calvin writes,

"On the other hand, it is evident that man never attains a
true self-knowledge until he has previously contemplated the
face of God, and come down after such contemplation to look
into himself."[22] Berkouwer sees in the Genesis passage that
"Man cannot truly know himself if he ignores the light of God's
revelation, which falls over his life, and which unveils the true
nature of man, of actual concrete man." [23]

If the notion of Calvin is accepted, and it seems to be a
reasonable understanding of self, then the relationship of this
self to God becomes the critical piece on which rests the whole
notion of the *Imago Dei*. For Emil Brunner, it becomes an answer to the tension of body and soul, and insight to a resolve
of a debate as old as humanity.[24]

In the examination of the text of Genesis it can be seen that
when the creation of humanity comes about, something strik-
ingly different seems to be implied. Brunner feels that com-
mentators who have pointed out a different quality in the text
concerning humanity's creation are entirely on target. He says,

> After the whole cosmos has come into existence, even if in dif-
> ferent ways, yet always under the same divine imperative: "And
> God said, Let there be and there was," it was as though the Lord
> of Creation paused for a while before the last great die was cast,
> and then began a new kind of creation.[25]

This new creation was stated so differently. It is, as Brunner
says, "a new creative act, and in this creative act, the creator
accomplishes his purpose as the Sistine Chapel ceiling depicts,
by stooping down."[26] Once humans have been made, it is clear
that they are made in both image and likeness of God.

Image and likeness are not to be divided (as was done by the
fathers and the Platonists) into a radical distinction based on
concreteness and abstraction that speak of creation separate

of body and soul. Nor is the distinction between the two to be
ignored as simply ancient semantics. No, the difference is to
modify the words so that in dual usage a singular idea of humanity can begin to appear. Humankind is *selem;* humanity
is image; humanity is replicas. Humanity is placed on earth
as God's representative; but it is not God, but *demuth,* a likeness of God. Humanity is, according to Psalm 8, a little lower
than the angels, but what gives it a special place is not just
the *selem* and *demuth* in a vacuum, but it is *selem* and *demuth*
as they relate to what humanity is to do, which is to have
dominion. Von Rad says,

> When, however, one has traced in a general way the distribution
> of weight in the Priestly account of man's creation, one will admit
> that the text speaks less of the nature of God's image than of its
> purpose. There is less said about the gift itself than about the task.
> This then is sketched most explicitly: domination in the world, es-
> pecially over the animals. This commission to rule is not considered
> as belonging to the definition of God's image; but it is its conse-
> quence, i.e., that for which man is capable because of it.[27]

It is C. F. D. Moule who adds a point that gives further clarity
to what von Rad has said, and ultimately to the position of this
book. He says, "Perhaps the most satisfying of the many interpretations, both ancient and modern, of the meaning of the
image of God in man is that which sees it basically as responsibility."[28] He goes on to say that even though God in his om-
nipotence has no forces with which he must check his powers,
he still wields his "authority responsibly." [29] In this particular
treatise Moule is relating the "responsible authority" to nature.
Stagg, however, also quotes Moule and expands responsible
authority from simply nature to all creation including other
beings who share the *Imago,* and he says, "To 'have dominion'
is to exercise responsible authority over things—this in the
company of God and other people." [30]

A Theology of Human Sexuality

It has been established from the discussion thus far that
biblical theology—to be correct—must hold to a body-soul oneness.

The body, contrary to the sentiment of some early Christian
writers, was made at the creation along with the psyche or soul
and shares with all that is man as recipient of the *Imago Dei.*
Stagg makes the case that *sarx,* commonly called "flesh," and
psyche, commonly called "spirit" or "self," are both words that

can be and are used to denote man as he is in his entirety.[31]

If logic is followed, then it must be concluded that the human body, including its procreative and sexual functioning, is included in the image and therefore cannot be viewed in any way as being inherently evil. Stagg says,

> Nowhere in Scripture is the human body itself seen as evil. This is a pagan concept, held by Gnostics and others; but it is not Biblical. In Biblical teaching, God created the heavens and the earth and all that is in them. He formed man's own body from the dust of the earth and breathed into it something of himself, thus making man a living soul.[32]

Following this notion, the words of von Rad serve as supportive witness when he comments on his own exegesis of Genesis 1:27:

> Sexual distinction is also created. The plural in verse 27 ("he created them") is intentionally contrasted with the singular ("him") and prevents one from assuming the creation of an originally androgynous man. By God's will, man was not created alone but designated for the "thous" of the other sex. The idea of man finds its full meaning not in male alone but in man and woman.[33]

In *Man in Revolt,* Brunner points out the problem of the sexes and sexuality as primarily one of the phenomenon of the problem of individuality. "A human being is individualized just as much by the fact of being male or female as by the fact that he or she belongs to a particular or has a peculiar physical 'make up.'" [34] He goes on to say, however, that sex, although individualized, goes much deeper than individuality. It goes into the core of human experience and is profoundly tied to the notion of *Imago Dei.* For Brunner it is through the *Imago* that Gnostic speculation is circumvented and arguments for asceticism and fear of sex allayed.[35] Brunner's concept is extremely important. Here in his notion of sexuality, as germane to individuality but then given perspective via *Imago Dei,* is a principle on which this book's development will stand. In the words of Stagg, humanity is "aspective yet holistic," and "individual yet corporate," [36] for in the true reception of a complete understanding of the meaning of *Imago Dei* (the understanding of sexuality and interdependence within creatureliness) it must be stated that "man finds his true existence in the polarity of solitude and solidarity, individuality and community." [37]

Summary

The image of God which is borne by all humanity certainly seems to turn on the axes of mutual responsibility, the duality of maleness and femaleness, and the relationship of creature to Creator. The authentic Judeo-Christian understanding of humanity has nothing to do with texture of hair, skin color, or other racial characteristics. Lifting those characteristics to norms of excellence came about through the Western world's attempts to revive the glories of ancient Greece.

For the millions of blacks who have been taught to hate themselves because their lips are too broad or their hair too kinky, this understanding of revelation is liberating. The sociological arguments over black family brokenness and female domination obscure what in the biblical revelation is wholeness.

To deal with the problems facing the black family, preachers, Christian educators, and theologians must begin their task with a thoroughgoing reaffirmation of the starting point for human community, which is the creation of humanity in God's image.

From every pulpit, in every classroom, and from the pen of every theologian must roll forth ceaseless attempts to overcome the satanic tendency in the Western world to align God's image with some romantic reminiscence of Greek culture.

The late sixties call that "black is beautiful" was a noble beginning. Where it did not go far enough was in grounding its truth in God's revelation and expanding the mosaic to include black is beautiful, yellow is beautiful, red is beautiful, and so forth. All racial features are merely particulars. Certainly none may be considered universally right. The universal nature of God's creation begins with a beauty which encompasses the uniqueness of every racial and ethnic type. It grounds desirability in humankind's being like God, not in our possessing only specific characteristics.

The questions of matriarchy also take on a completely new meaning when the revelation is turned to as a source for interpreting sexuality. Slavery permitted an equality of the sexes which was based on mutual pain. The sharing of pain was and has been a source for the solidarity of black males and females.

In the relationship of the male to the female the black family has experienced itself as a suffering community. The cold realities of whips and chains and slave catchers never permitted men to treat their women as dolls. Rape by whites, total denial of respect, and little or no access to privacy prevented women from developing any romantic notion of self. Husbands, wives, and children shared fully in being denied their humanity. In many ways it was this perception of the essential black identity being that of a suffering community which permitted the slaves to identify so closely with Jesus. To them he was the sweet little Jesus boy who had his image defined as sufferer by no fault of his own. The biblical Jesus and the slaves all joined vicariously in this fellowship of agony.

An offshoot of this mutual suffering was that blacks did not have the luxury of denying their sexual roles as being mutual, as originally intended by God. In fact, in spite of the social scientists' assessment of the male as irresponsible, the shared suffering of the black family kept alive the notion of mutual responsibility. Through mutual responsibility the black family learned adaptation as a survival skill. The patriarchal power games of the European settlers were denied the slaves. The slaves could not allow women to be put on pedestals and treated like children. The sharing of suffering saw to it that for a family to survive, the woman had to do what was necessary. If her jobs were dehumanizing, so be it. The family did not have time to debate what constituted women's work. Black women split logs, worked in the fields, worked on road gangs, and kept the master's house, as a step toward the greater good, which was the black family's survival.

What Moynihan and sociologists have completely misunderstood is that what white European society calls "matriarchy," black folks call "staying alive." It is to the credit of blacks in America that through the family's shared pain, the black woman emerged without many of the "weaker sex" stereotypes that have been inherited by significant numbers of white females.

The image of God is a concept with which the church can teach persons of all ages dignity, respect, and mutual responsibility. These concepts have been successfully taught by black Muslims, without the aid of the Christian church's influence in the black community, for years. Their successes in prisons and in some of the fiercest ghettos in this country are an indication that blacks are looking for a reordering of their self-understanding which makes them reach for authentic community beyond the hustling, the dope pushing, and the crime. The image of God is an image where the macho games of trying to get over on others has no place. Pure mutuality means men as well as women share in the work of child rearing and child care. One cannot respect another until one has learned to respect oneself. In this culture, the plethora of negative images which flood television, radio, movies, and theatre make our culture an impossible place for a young black to understand who he or she is.

The church is a place where the revaluing of self-image can occur. In the church, role modeling can be accomplished and dignity cannot only be taught but caught. Persons may be moved to see that being made in the image of God mandates the abnegation of sexual role stereotypes and encourages a mutual responsibility which affords nurturing for the young, protection for the aged, and belonging for the homeless. The original image of God can then be understood to encompass the important aspects of dominion. Through an understanding of what it means for persons to have dominion, a newly developed sense of ecology can develop. This ecological sense affords a source out of which respect for self and respect for others leads to a respect for every aspect of God's creation.

4

Families—Sharing in
the Image of God

In chapter 3 the biblical concept of personhood was explored as a way of developing an introduction and a theological perspective based on the family. The next step in the process is to move to a recognition of "partnering" as the soul of covenantal relationships. This section is critical to the overall development of a family-based theology because partnering and covenant provide the link from the self to society, relationships, and others.

The relationship of maleness and femaleness has been a theme throughout the discussion of God's image. When one comes to the task of relating, however, other questions must be raised. Maleness and femaleness are equal portions of the original image of God shared by humanity, but interrelatedness implies a sense of covenant. It moves us from discussions of personhood to discussions of partnering, from maleness and femaleness in the abstract to male and female as individual entities.

To understand the uniqueness of partnering from a black perspective, we must examine the history and traditions of the African family. As has been mentioned, African family structure is often much more consanguineal than conjugal. For that reason, partnering in the black context must be understood much more broadly than in a purely nuclear arrangement. An African family member historically was partner in a number of arenas. There was the partnership between husband and wife, between other adults of the consanguineal family, be-

tween the grandparents and children, and between the living
and the dead. In fact, humankind was seen as being fully in
partnership with the entirety of the created order. The African
family system was marked by a general sharing within family
and between partners that was much different from the European paradigm.

The question must be raised, however, of the relationship of
revelation (i.e., Scripture) to the African family system. Again,
my contention is that any attempt to strengthen the black
family system must take its source from the universality of
biblical truth, not from any system of philosophy or science.

The question, then, is what in the revelation points us toward
the extended family as a model of God's interrelationship with
humankind?

First, in the reality of the Trinity we encounter a God who
is in relationship with self. A basic understanding of our relationship takes on profound theological significance when God
is seen as a God both of and in relationship with God's self and
with the creation.

Second, the extended family concept seems to be supported
by the biblical understanding of covenant. Abraham is the
faithful covenant partner. It is his faithfulness which enables
him to go in search of a city and have the assurance that the
gods of other areas and cities had no control over him as long
as his oracles were from the God who is not bound by space or
time. The covenant of faithfulness was not only just a covenant
with Abraham; it was also a covenant with Abraham's offspring. All his descendants who simply remained faithful to
the original covenant had the profound assurance that their
father's God would in turn be faithful to them.

With the coming of Christ, the concept of the extended family
became even more firmly rooted in the church doctrine. Equal
access to the Lord's Supper provided a way of being adopted
into the family of God. Now, the membership into the family
was not through blood ties but through affinity of spirit. Baptism becomes the new birth, and all who took Jesus' lordship
as their point of orientation were assured that same promise
of God's steadfast love as those faithful blood descendants of
Abraham.

There is in the biblical revelation, then, a very strong sense of extended family. This is important for the unraveling of negative stereotypes and also for the shoring up of black self-image. Female-centered families must not be automatically viewed as sick, especially when the basis of that assessment is a European nuclear family ideal. An extended family system where older brothers, uncles, or grandparents are present may provide the male role models needed to afford male and female children the nurturing necessary for proper emotional health.

Attitudes are critical in the successful implementation of any activity. This is why so much time must be spent in reestablishing the image of God in the hearts and minds of blacks throughout society.

Blacks in this country live consistently below the economic level of whites. The economic realities tend to exacerbate all other problems. To cope, blacks have often turned to the extended family for help. The following statement establishes a telling reality:

> In a study, Dubey (1971) examined the relationship between self-alienation and extended family using black, white and Puerto Rican subjects. The data supported the hypotheses that subjects with a high degree of powerlessness were significantly more oriented toward the extended family. Dubey's study raises the question of whether the extended family is used as a buffer between oppression of the dominant society and the unmet needs of the family.[1]

Elmer P. Martin and Joanne Mitchell Martin have written a very insightful book entitled *The Black Extended Family*. The contention is ultimately that the black extended family is not either an expression of "strength resilence or of pathology-disorganization" [2] but expresses both concepts. Their feeling is that the extended family model did not survive simply because the family was so broken by slavery. Nor does the extended family exist merely as a noble expression of African retentions and strength resiliency. It exists as a combination of these factors, but the essential reality is that the extended family for Afro-Americans, for whatever reason, is ascendant to the nuclear arrangement.

Martin and Martin define an extended family as possessing

[1] Jualynne Dodson, "Conceptualizations of Black Families," p. 29 in *Black Families,* edited by Harriet McAdoo. Copyright © 1981 by Sage Publications, Inc. Reprinted by permission of Sage Publications, Inc.

the following characteristics:

> First, it is interdependent. Relatives depend on one another for
> emotional, social, and most importantly, material support. Second,
> it is multigenerational, consisting of four generations of relatives.
> Third, it is headed by a dominant family figure. Fourth, it has an
> extended family base household, which is always the residence of
> the dominant family figure. Fifth, it reaches across geographical
> boundaries. Sixth, it has a built-in mutual aid system for providing
> material and moral support for family members.[3]

Let us examine two critical issues raised out of these definitions. First, the dominant family member is quite often a
woman. This must not be used, however, as a way to denigrate
the image of the black family as a matriarchy.

> A family with a female as the head appears to be a female-dominated
> or matriarchal household, when in fact, several male relatives may
> be influential in such a household setting. An uncle, a male cousin,
> an older brother, a boyfriend, or even a grandmother or aunt could
> be a father figure to the children.[4]

Second, for Afro-American people, the extended family also
acted as a mutual aid system. Economic pressures again must
be weighed in every discussion of the black family. Black people
from the time of slavery had first and foremost to deal with
finding the resources simply to stay alive. The kinship network
provided a way for resources to be shared. Within the family,
matters of education, weddings, and health care were dealt
with through the mutual sharing of a family's goods and resources.

The dominant culture's denigrations of the black family system come out of white America's romance with rugged individualism. To the conqueror of the plains and the subjugator
of the Native American, a man's man was someone who took
care of his family first, asked for no help and was up to whatever
violence was necessary to insure that self and family dignity
were not violated. The folly of that cowboy mentality is that
the dominant culture was, of course, the recipient of a number
of welfare programs. Slave labor certainly fits that bill. The
capital generated throughout this nation through access to millions of free laborers is staggering. The thinly disguised slavery
of the coolie wages paid to orientals in the late nineteenth
century was another welfare giveaway. So, too, was the original

homesteading act which allowed persons to advance into entrepreneurship through the simple act of staking claim to land that was free if you were white. It must never be forgotten that it was not rugged individualism, but theft of this land from the indigenous peoples through colonialism which is foundational to the power and influence of American capitalism.

The black family's mutual aid networking is not unique in this society. It was simply a carryover from Africa of a tribal structure that blacks felt comfortable with which allowed them a mutual support system. This mutual support network is of the utmost importance when it is realized that in the face of the genocide and unspeakable holocaust perpetrated against people of color, the extended family was the only place blacks could turn to for support.

The System of Adoption

The black family has developed as an adoptive and absorptive entity. The image of God is reflected by the image in humankind of mutual respect, and ecological responsibility is practiced in the black family in the care of the elderly and in the practice of informal adoptions. "Family members who are homeless or unable to care for themselves for reasons of age, sickness, unemployment, or whatever may be taken into the household of a relative. This 'absorption mechanism' is an important facet of the mutual aid system within the black extended family." [5] Persons in need are provided an opportunity to be a part of another's family structure, if their family is either unwilling or unable to provide care and nurture.

This adoption begins with locating a home for the needy. The process of extending the boundaries of one's home to the homeless may take place for a few weeks, it may take place for a few years, or it may eventuate in a permanent arrangement.

This absorption occurs at a much higher rate for children than adults[6] and comes about as a result of a family or family member's inability to provide for offspring.

This phenomenon was particularly common during the mass migration from the South between 1900 and 1929. This period has been called the Great Northern Drive. During this time, the black population of New York increased by ninety-one thousand, Chicago by seventy-nine thousand, Philadelphia by seventy-three thousand and Detroit by thirty-six thousand. The migration, signaled by a southern boll weevil blight and continued systemic violence inflicted on blacks by whites, left many blacks without the resources to care for their families.

A typical scenario of this period was for a mother or a father to leave the children with a relative or close friend who remained in the South, as they came North in search of employment. Once employment was found and the economic situation eased, children were sent for. Many children, however, basically received their essential rearing through these surrogate parents because the process of getting situated up North was often a long and bitter one. Many of the parents in the North found economic realities in the ghetto as harsh if not more harsh than on the farm. For many, the dream of being free— even in the North—never occurred.

The black family's ability to adopt and absorb was an adaptive skill which, for all the negative results ultimately, did manage to keep blacks alive through the long winters and hot summers of economic disaster and racial unrest.

This adoptive absorptive system, unfortunately, also produced some alienation and disenfranchisement amongst families. Sibling rivalries were heightened by the realities of which one of the children Momma or Daddy chose to take with them and which one stayed South to live with aunts and uncles. Some bitter family disputes lasted generations after the fact, but the essential reality remained that through this adaptive skill black families did manage to stay alive. The soul of the black adoptive system, however, is male/female partnering. From this base emerged the mutual aid and adoptive systems that typify the black extended family.

The Image of God and Marriage

If the African extended family is to be strengthened, the sexual unions formed within the family must have some guidelines upon which to draw. Questions of matriarchy versus patriarchy must be dealt with as well as headship versus mutuality and monogamy versus polygamy. To answer these questions, let us look at some of the biblical images of marriage.

And Pharisees came up and in order to test him asked, "Is it lawful for a man to divorce his wife?" He answered them, "What did Moses command you?" They said, "Moses allowed a man to write a certificate of divorce, and to put her away." But Jesus said to them, "For your hardness of heart he wrote you this commandment. But from the beginning of creation, 'God made them male and female.' 'For this reason a man shall leave his father and mother and be joined to his wife, and the two shall become one flesh" (Mark 10:2-8, RSV).

In this passage Jesus quotes the portion of the *Imago Dei* concerning maleness and femaleness. He says that from the beginning God made them this way and seems to be saying that both are coequal aspects of the *image*. From the fact that Jesus quotes this as the goal of marriage relationships, a clear understanding of what is implied is of utmost importance. It may be recalled that the original statement of Genesis 1:26-27 (RSV) is "God said, let us make man (*adham*). . .them."

The *image* in its original conception is one of *adham,* humankind being created in the image of God. Jesus' refutation of wanton divorce laws serves as a reminder to the Pharisees that the *image* is, "from the beginning." It is not something tacked on at some later date with lesser significance. It also cannot be said that the body, i.e., human sexuality, was not part of the *image* because Jesus quotes that very portion from Genesis 1:27 which asserts that maleness and femaleness are from the beginning how God made them. He then seems to say what was a radical statement: maleness and femaleness are oneness. "For this reason a man shall leave his father and mother and be joined to his wife, and the two shall become one flesh" (Mark 10:7-8, RSV). For "one" Jesus uses the Semitic idiom *mia sarx,* "one flesh."

Even though *sarx* can mean humankind generically, its use here takes on more profundity if in using the idiom for "oneness," Jesus actually did intend to suggest that "fleshliness" "corporality," has a significant slice of the *image* tied to it (i.e., of maleness and femaleness). There is no hard evidence to support *mia sarx* being anything but "one," but the speculation still has merit in that maleness and femaleness in the creation accounts are related to the *Imago Dei.*

Another New Testament aspect of the *Imago Dei* is the way it is used by Paul, especially pertaining to the notion of "headship," "for the husband is the head of the wife as Christ is the head of the church, his body, and is himself its Savior" (Ephesians 5:23, RSV). With the concept of headship, Paul really says a great deal about the *Imago Dei* as he understood it. (Some of the interpretations may be startling, and it is indeed a shame that so many have undertaken work on marriage and the family without ever trying to understand what the *Imago Dei* really means to Paul's concept of headship.) To understand Ephesians 5:23 one must also have the sense of the meaning of 5:21 and 5:22.

Marcus Barth translated Ephesians 5:21 as, "Because you fear Christ."[7] He says that his form of referring to Christ is rare in the New Testament and because of its difficult theological implications, many have shunned "fear" for a softer interpretation.[8]

To Barth, this fear aspect solves a very basic problem; for the bridging of the gap between the rigid subordination idea of Ephesians 5:21-23 and the more universal understanding of 1 Corinthians 7. He goes on to say that the *"haustefel"* or household duties are really keyed in the concept in verse 22 of mutual subordination (that is for husbands and wives and children); and that the mutuality of the subordination is intricately entwined with a Pauline system of eschatology which is revealed more fully in 1 Corinthians 7.[9]

He makes this point because his research has unearthed the fact that some manuscripts will add the imperative "subordinate yourselves" in verse 22 or "shall be subjected" as an interpretative device that unfortunately obscures the concept of mutual subjection and therefore by inference implies a natural order to male superiority and female inferiority.[10] From this springboard, Barth makes a point which is crucial in the understanding of the *Imago Dei* (as it applies to maleness and femaleness). The literal translation "For the husband is the head of the wife as Christ is the head of the church" reduces the Messiah to a "secondary example." [11]

> Indeed Paul could not have been ignorant of the fact that a majority of married people of this time followed a pattern of behavior which attributed superior responsibility to the husband and inferior positions to the wife; also he must have known that this pattern was considered by many perfectly reasonable and adequate—without being informed by Jesus Christ's love for the church.[12]

The basic question here is whether or not Paul adds the relationship of Christ to the church as a superfluous addendum to support existing customs, or did he add it to show a uniqueness, from the headship of Christ, that ought to be applied to the headship of husband over wife? If, as the New Testament passages seem to consistently imply, Christ never was given as protector of natural customs, then perhaps there is here a startling but perceptive new understanding of headship, i.e., that "Jesus Christ is the only cause and standard for the saints' conduct," [13] an understanding that rests on a critical interpretation of the vocabulary in the verse.

Barth translates *hos kai ho christos* in the unusual but extremely profound way as "only in Christ," which gives the fuller interpretation this sense.

"Because you fear Christ subordinate yourselves to one another [e.g., wives to your husbands] as to the Lord. For [only] in the same way that the Messiah is the head of the church—he, the savior of his body—is the husband the head of his wife" (Ephesians 5:21-23).[14]

A Theology of Marriage

At first glance, strict biblical interpretation of such passages as Ephesians 5:21–6:4 makes all but the patriarchal nuclear family (as classically defined) unacceptable. This kind of data must be understood in its broader cultural context; and just as no one of any degree of intelligence would accept the definition of the master-slave relationship in these passages as normative and desirable, the existence of present-day cultural considerations must also weigh on the strict interpretation of the husband-wife dyad as normative. What is normative in these passages is the spirit of their intent. That spirit seems to be the overwhelming notion that the quality of life is based on the quality of relationships. Although the husband-wife dyad may be the ideal for family life, the counter notion that all other family experience is deviant and therefore unstable is an unacceptable thesis. The spirit of these passages and their intent seems to lie in the basic assumption that the quality of life is made better by a relationship with Christ that allows for total subjection to the needs of others and total respect for the uniqueness of others. God intends for Christians to live in unity,

Paul seems to be saying in Ephesians 4:1-6, and this is done by the nurturing of all the specific gifts of those who are members of the body. In Galatians 3:26-28 (RSV), we find, "For in Christ Jesus you are all sons of God, through faith. For as many of you as were baptized into Christ have put on Christ. There is neither Jew or Greek, there is neither slave nor free, there is neither male nor female; for you are all one in Christ Jesus."

What he is stating for women is that there is to be new status found in Christ Jesus. That analogy can be carried over into the family structure. For the Christian family there is new life in Christ Jesus, new life which does not place the excellency of any given family on adherence to roles, but places its excellency on the strengthened relationships of those family members who have mutually subjected themselves to Christ, mutually pledged respect for their own specific uniqueness, and mutually worked toward the building of positive self-images.

For many, however, the passage in Ephesians is a troubling one: "For the husband is the head of the wife as Christ is the head of the church, his body, and is himself its Savior (5:23, RSV). The passage at first reading seems uncomfortable because it seems to state so definitively Paul's concept of the husband-wife relationship. Heinrich Schlier, in the *Theological Dictionary of the New Testament,* looks at the Greek word which is translated as "head." He says that the head is not present without or apart from the body, nor the body without or apart from the head. The Church is the earthly body of the heavenly head. In this unity of Christ and the church, the headship of Christ is manifested in the fact that he directs the growth of the body to himself.[15] This understanding makes critical the idea of growth. The head determines the being of the body and the fulfillment of its life. As the head, Christ is the concrete principle of the bodily growth of the church. Schlier's definition, when applied to the present-day family, would remove the essentiality of economic viability in a definition of the man as the head of the family. Growth of the unit and wholeness of the family unit are not contingent upon the economic leadership of the male. The translation of Markus Barth of Ephesians 5:23 adds a great deal of insight to the question of headship. Barth's translation provides a radical break from the legalistic and pagan perspectives of headship implying patriarchate, i.e., male dominance. The husband is head "only" as Christ is head, and Christ's headship is not demonstrated by dominance but by subjection, both to others and to God. This also adds a fresh perspective to the account in Mark 10:2-8. The question is not the power question of whether or not husbands have the right to put away their wives. The question is the love ethic question, resolved by maleness and femaleness being a part of the "image of God," coequal, co-responsible, and co-dependent upon each other.[16]

A family is not matriarchal simply because it does not meet certain standards. It is not broken simply because the male is not in the position of economic leadership. Black sociologists have repeatedly taken the position that the black male's economic frailty is not based on inherent ineptness or inaptitude; it is instead based on a rigorous racism that has permeated all levels of the American cultural psyche, as is demonstrated by the monthly unemployment statistics.

> The most striking feature of African family and community life was the strong and dominant place in family and society assigned to and assumed by the men. This strong, masculine dominance, however, far from being capricious authoritarianism, was supported, guided, and limited by custom and tradition which also provided a substantial role for the women. The children were provided a quality of care and protection not common in modern society, for they belonged not alone to their father and mother, but also, and principally, to the wider kinship group.[17]

In *Man as Male and Female,* Paul K. Jewett explored an idea that helps to focus the whole question (theologically) of male-female interdependence.

> There are, broadly speaking, three schools of thought about the sexual polarity of man's existence, which are neglected at least to some degree, in representative Christian writers. First of all, there is the position that the male-female distinction has nothing to contribute to our understanding of man as created in the divine image. A second view affirms that while the male-female distinction is not an essential part of the doctrine of man, it is evident from Scripture that both male and female share the distinct endowments whereby man differs from animals; that is to say that men and woman both participate in the divine image. According to a third view, to be in the image of God is to be male and female.[18]

Nicholai Berdyaev, a writer holding to the first view, feels that the polar nature of maleness and femaleness is due to humanity's fallen nature. He sees human fulfillment only in the union of the personal anthropological principles which are masculine with the communal and cosmic principles which are feminine. A theologian of the more traditional second view is Emil Brunner, who treats the question of man in the divine image as distinct from the question of man as male and female. "Brunner does not have a theology of sexuality which would make the man/woman distinction essential to humanity." [19]

Brunner's anthropology really sees sexuality, and no marriage, as the touchstone of the male-female question. His theology merges the question of what the Christian understanding is of man as male and female with the question of what the Christian understanding is of the roles which the male and female have to fill respectively in the ordinance of marriage. His answer is that sexual dualism is neither to be played down nor glorified. The ultimate fulfillment is in the life to come when we shall forever be like God, with emphasis being placed on Mark 12:25: "At the resurrection of the dead they neither marry nor are given in marriage, but are like the angels in heaven" (paraphrased).

The third view, as articulated by Karl Barth, assumes that the concept of man and woman is tied to the concept of the *Imago Dei*. Genesis 1:27 (RSV) says, "So God created man in his own image, in the image of God created he him, male and female created he them." Barth's position is that we never say "mankind" without having to say either "man" or "woman." Man has his existence based precisely on this distinction. In all human uniqueness, persons are still either male or female. For Barth, man in the ultimate sense is both male and female.

Man is male and female, and the concept of man in the image of God lies in that unity. Sexuality is not some incidental footnote to life; it is the core of existence—one side of this duality has no meaning without the concurrent other side. Karl Barth, much more than some other theologians, has developed a doctrine which forces one to develop a theology of man which is also a theology of woman.[20]

While in a Nazi prison camp, Dietrich Bonhoeffer wrote a wedding sermon which captures the richness of the concept in marriage of responsibility to each other but also of responsibility to humankind:

> "Marriage is more than your love for each other. It has a higher dignity and power, for it is God's holy ordinance through which He wills to perpetuate the human race till the end of time. In your love you see only your two selves in the world, but in marriage you are a link in the chain of generations, which God causes to come and to pass away to His glory, and calls into His kingdom. In your love you see only the heaven of your happiness, but in marriage you are placed at a post of responsibility towards the world and mankind. Your love is your own private possession, but marriage is more than something personal—it is a status; an office."[21]

The points that Bonhoeffer raises are important. Christian marriage does have a profound significance and sanctity. The New Testament is moving us to see how the progressive nature of God's revelation has reached a zenith for interpersonal communication in the office of marriage. Unlike the ancient customs, Christian marriage forces persons to see women not as chattel but as full participators in the original image of God. Therefore women are not to be treated as objects or believed to exist simply to satisfy men. Christian marriage raises women to a level of dignity which was unheard of in antiquity.

Christian marriage lifts up mutual sacrifice as the *sine quo non* of human relationships. Marriage is to reflect the mutual subjection that demands of each partner full loving sacrifice to the other. This does not mean that individuality is lost. It means that a new sense of identity is found when one is willing to give totally. Much as the carpenter from Nazareth became Jesus the Christ through his obedience unto the cross, in mutual sacrifice persons are transformed into a unique oneness of body and mind.

Marriage requires that persons pledge themselves in full trust to the other. This cannot be done as an idle notion. It must be done with the full understanding that by pledging one's self, one is also pledging one's life.

As Bonhoeffer points out, this new shared sense of responsibility is an office. By accepting the responsibility of marriage one is showing forth that he or she is accepting a unique but vital responsibility.

By the same token, a single lifestyle is not second-class citizenship. There is a nobility which also can be a part of a single life if other aspects of mutual responsibility are accepted. The genius of the extended family permits that possibility.

The office of marriage, however, is an office in which two persons accept the church's sanction to bring new life into the world. At this point the marital office is indeed unique and its responsibilities of a different order than that of the single person.

The Christian marriage is marked biblically by pure mutuality, sacrifice, love (in its highest form) and exclusivity. These concepts all culminate in the doctrine of one flesh.

The Image of God and Female/Male Relationships

In attempting to establish revelation as the basis of a theology of the black family, the question of female/male interrelatedness must be raised. The extended family concept notwithstanding, one must come to grips with the image of God as it relates to males and females and the nature of the marital covenant. A knowledge and appreciation of the consanguineal family structure of western Africa has tremendous potential to help and heal black families. A knowledge of one's roots, as Alex Haley brilliantly displayed, is a very liberating phenomenon. On the heels of that knowledge of history, however, blacks must also have a deep appreciation for the directions in which God's revelation is pointing. Ultimately and finally there is no authentic liberation outside of God's revelation.

The image of God is rounded out as an image of male-female interrelatedness. Each of us individually is both male and female, but each is also specifically male or female. God's revelation clearly points to male-female monogamous relationships as the gift given by God to humankind for the purposes of procreation and nurturing. Even for people of African descent, this concept of monogamy must be at the heart of even the extended family structure.

For African peoples the polygamous system grew up out of the frequent wars that insured that female survival rates were higher than male. Polygamy was a way to insure a high birth rate. This system was accepted as a way of insuring that women would not become spinsters and therefore lose the potential for child bearing. Polygamy also was a way of preventing a proliferation of prostitution.

The rather high rate of common-law marriages among blacks in this country is a vestige of the African polygamous system. Some in this country today still argue for polygamy as an alternative to the deliberate murder practiced upon black people and to the still much higher rates of eligible females to males because of the disproportionately high percentages of black males who are imprisoned, compared to the ethnic constitution of American society. Such practices are seen as necessary for the survival of a people.

These problems are problems which certainly must be dealt with, but an understanding of the revelation of God certainly indicates that polygamous marriages are not a part of the created image of God. Male and female in deep and abiding partnership is the only authentic way that one can read Genesis 1:26-27. When other lifestyles are adopted, it must be understood that those lifestyles do not reflect the clearest response that can be given to God's will. Black leaders, teachers, and preachers must be about the task of developing national strategies that deal with the need for drastic prison reforms as well as better nutrition, better prenatal care, and effective job training for the developing job markets as ways of improving the black birth rate and insuring that blacks have an equal access to a fair share of the American dream. That kind of leadership must be performed at the same time that monogamous committed marriage is being taught. Only when blacks have the opportunity to align themselves totally with God's intentions will liberation be an actual possibility.

5

Toward a Family
Ministry

The question now is "What can the churches do to maximize the potential of the black family?" This question is a critical one in light of the sobering statistics which point out time and again that the plight of the black family in many ways is worse today than it was ten years ago.

Sociologist Charles V. Willie, speaking at a meeting of the National Council of the Churches of Christ, said that to aid the extraordinary problems of the family "society should be spending less time on the structure of the family questions like divorce, marriage and number of children and more time on finding ways of helping families create warm, loving environments." [1]

In this talk, Willie contrasted warm households where people were reared to feel good about themselves to cool households where people grow up feeling either negative or neutral about themselves.

Interesting reversals take place, according to Willie, depending on one's social class and status. Middle-class white families hold the goal of individuality as the highest good. Middle-class blacks, however, put more emphasis on curbing personal freedom for the good of the whole. Among the poor, however, it is whites who exalt the family while blacks exalt the individual.

J. Deotis Roberts says,

When the black church is viewed as a family, all persons, whether married, single, or divorced will come to a sense of kinship in the church as the family of God. The church is the family under the lordship of Jesus Christ to whom all families in heaven and earth owe their substance and health. Let us hasten the day when the church will be a family and the family a domestic church. Then will God's kingdom be nearer than we had believed.[2]

In making this statement, Roberts is summing up the potential of the black family to provide a model for church ecclesiology and the potential of the black church to act as a caring and healing place for broken families.

A black family theology has something to contribute to white, black, affluent, or poor communities. Black family theology grew out of the roots of the African tribal system. It did not stop there, however. Black theology generally is a mixture of the slavery experience, the African indigenous religions, and the Judeo-Christian experience. Black family theology adds to the concept of black theology the notion of ecclesiology. Black family theology is not an abstract philosophical system. It is not an intellectual debate over issues of liberation. It is an actual practice of theology, a coming together of God's people for the purpose of doing God's will and in so doing functioning as God's community.

The black church in America retains its vitality against extraordinary odds because it was born as an expression of the black extended family. The ancient tribal structure of Africa was used and improved upon. The consanguineal family models of western Africa were drawn on for inspiration. The black church is an extended family. The pastor functions as chief and male parent. The first lady (or if the pastor is single, a senior mother of the church) functions as female parent. The governing board of deacons, elders, or presbyters functions as the older adults in the consanguineal unit, and the membership at large functions as the siblings.

With this concept in mind, the black church does have a theology which not only has potential to deal with the problems of black folk, but also has a theology which potentially can educate persons of all races to the potential warmth a church can develop if that church begins to understand how it has potential to function as an extended family.

For this to happen, persons must begin to rethink the very concept of the organized church. An extended family theology must challenge a position basic to much of modern pastoral theology, namely, that of clergy professionalism. In the black church the clergy person attempts to exhibit a measure of professionalism, but ultimately he or she is not an executive, but the family's parent. As the family's parent he or she is expected to show parental love, care, and time for the family. The following, a tribute delivered at a pastor's twenty-fifth anniversary during a morning worship service, illustrates this point.

A Tribute to Dad

To God Be the Glory

It is indeed a befitting theme for our [the church's] seventieth anniversary. Because nothing but a good and humble Dad could have maintained a family of this magnitude for the last twenty-five years. However, being children, how easily do we forget! So we would like to jog your memory to see how well do we remember.

How well do we remember! It seemed like yesterday that you, Dad, a quiet but gentle warrior headed Zion's way; perhaps on your first visit you had no intention to stay. But our Heavenly Father was well aware that our Pastor was going away. He looked among his children, for there were other Sons. But with a quiet and gentle voice He said, "Coleman, you are the Chosen One. To guide the old ship of Zion, for there will be many toils and snares. But if you keep your hand in God's hand, there is a bright side somewhere."

Praise God for Pastor Gregory. Before he left the sands of time, he placed you, Dad, at the head of the table. To preach, to sup, and to dine. How well do we remember the day the wedding came—when you, Dad, together with Mount Zion became synonymous as one name. How do we remember how your children came! The Brotherhood Chorus, the Gospelheirs, the Carnation, how they learned the songs of Zion and are continuously praising his name. A few of your family members, namely Sisters Anna K. Smith, Edna Rucker, Mamie Mallory, and Brother Leonard Loper saw a need and had the will to nurture and develop some of your young and named them the Christian Culture Guild.

How well do we remember, for we always were told to welcome our friends and neighbors, both young and old, into the family.

It mattered not where they were going or where they had been; perhaps after hearing one of your sermons they might stay. So Deacon Cornelius Evans organized the New Members Friends Club.

Your society of daughters and missionaries, they are welcomed by Sister Lucille Kilebrew into the family business, and as professional women they are serving mankind near and far.

Well, Dad, your family is twenty-five years older but still at the head of the table you sit. We, your children, here at Mount Zion honor and love you with all love and respect. Your family will continue to grow more and more each day. Your many grandchildren are just a prayer away. Along with your sons, namely Rev. Sidney Mills, Wallace Smith, Raymond Baylor, Timothy Ruffin, Keith Reid, and Harry Collins you have developed with your quiet and gentle way. We are here paying tribute to you, Dad, on this, your special day. May God ever Bless you and keep you in his care.

With fondest memories, one of your children,

Bette Stevenson[3]

Edward P. Wimberly says,

The black pastor has been expected, as a symbol of the community, to help the person in crisis find meaning for his or her existence. Often the expectation has been that the pastor would provide specific advice and direction to the person. In some instances, the pastor was expected to take over and take charge. This taking-over function is called parenting.[4]

In many ways the parenting roles of the pastor and first lady are critical to the warmth of the rest of the family. As with the nuclear family, the Ephesians concept of headship is again appropriate. The pastor and first lady, as heads of the church, have the responsibility to direct the growth of the organism. In another tribute read at the same service at Mount Zion a young man included these words:

I remember one time when I was little, Rev. Coleman came to my house for Christmas dinner. I sat between him and Mrs. Coleman, and after he said the blessing, my mother put collard greens on my plate. At the time, I couldn't stand collard greens and I had no intentions of eating them. Mrs. Coleman looked at me and said, "Damone, you'd better eat those greens if you want to grow up to be like Rev." So, I've been eating collard greens ever since. So this shows you how influential Rev. Coleman has been to my life.[5]

Of course, the caution that must be added is that parenting when insensitively performed may degenerate into paternalism or matriarchy. The black church as had its share of pastors who confused fatherly parenting with totalitarian autocracy and first ladies who viewed themselves as supreme rulers of the roost. Those extremes must be avoided; when they are not, churches are extremely susceptible to splits and disruptions. In the earlier chapters that dealt with the extended family, the point was raised that often one person, usually an older female, is responsible for the coordination of the family's life. Many first ladies free their pastor/husbands up for other ministerial functions such as social action because they have assumed these responsibilities. In our rapidly changing world the role functioning of clergy and spouse is not always as clearly defined as it once was. Once churches expected the first lady to function in a matriarchal capacity. Although that expectation may still exist on the part of churches, many clergy spouses are pursuing careers of their own and no longer want to take their dominant sense of self-worth from their husband's employment. The changing of roles among spouses as well as the rise of female clergy are items which will necessitate rethinking some of the classical role definitions of the parenting function of pastor and first lady (or first man) in the black church extended family structure.

The functioning of the church elders in the family must also be understood as a family office, not as purely an administrative post. In the black Baptist conventions deacons are still ordained to their posts. This is done as a way for the church family to bestow senior status upon them. The church is saying to them: "We view you in a unique role. You are to be counselors to our pastor/parent. Your job is to see that he or she is able to effectively perform the tasks of ministry, and you are to be the ones who keep your attentions upon us. You are to miss us when we do not come to church. You are to attend to us when we are sick. You are to provide role models for the young by being persons to look up to and to respect."

The function of the lay membership is also in keeping with the family paradigm. As with siblings in the family, some people will be shy, some aggressive, some quite capable, and others in need of encouragement. The dynamics of these relationships are important for a well-rounded, healthy church family. As family, there is the general sharing in the Word which is the spiritual food necessary for survival. The family of God will come to the table at the time of worship to eat together the Lord's Supper, rejoice together in birth (baptism or infant dedication), weep together in death, and work together to build a new (church) home when the old one is no longer sufficient.

As the family of God, the church shares several basic qualities with black families generally. The first of these is that to be black in America is still to be a sufferer. The statistics bear this fact out. Black people are still underemployed, still experience poor medical care, and still basically live in communities characterized by substandard housing. Secondly, the black church is an inclusive community. Although the titular heads of many churches are male, the basic reality is that women share the power in the black church. If anything, the increasingly larger ratios of women to men in churches are creating a problem of balance in the role modeling for young people. Thirdly, the black church is an adoptionist community. Unlike other churches, the black church has historically been willing to accept into the membership persons who were outside the fold. Once accepted, these persons were treated as full participants in the life of and the decision-making functions of the church.

A Praxis for Black Family Theology

Cornell West's contention was that the basic problems facing blacks are self-identity and self-determination. Black family theology provides a model for effective church functioning, which maximizes the utilization of the church's goods and resources.[6]

I mentioned earlier that the parenting function may degenerate into a totalitarian autocracy. All cultures can be greatly helped by developing an ecclesiology which is built on the ideal of the black extended family. The African roots of the black extended family point very clearly to the fact that administration of the well-being of the tribe was not a chiefly unilateral responsibility, but a mutual responsibility. The base of the tribe's life was the mutuality with which decisions were made. Elders, chiefs, wives, and children all had voices in the decision-making process. The denial of a voice to any member of the family is not an African but a Western tradition. The praxis of black family theology is built upon the principles of mutuality of suffering, inclusion, adoption, and hope.

The development of actual programs which will address the problems of the black family must be done in light of societal realities facing the black family. These realities are that as a suffering community blacks in America are significantly worse off than whites in the areas of health care, jobs, education, and housing.

Maslow in his landmark work in psychology develops what has come to be called the "hierarchy of needs." [7] His work is quite valuable in helping to discover a beginning point at which family enrichment must begin for blacks.

What he says, in effect, is that human need is arranged in a pyramid fashion and that each level higher on the pyramid can only be attained when the lower ones have been sufficiently addressed. A sketch of his paradigm appears below.

The valuable information this theory provides is that if blacks are still basically struggling at the physiological level, the other higher levels cannot be successfully achieved. Self-actualization is virtually impossible to attain if one is struggling to find the resources to pay bills, buy food, and receive adequate rest.

This pyramid indicates an important revision in the latter

transcendence

self-
actualization

truth
Good News
beauty
aliveness
individuality
justice
order

self-esteem
esteem by others

love
belongingness

safety
security

physiological:
air, water, food, shelter, sleep, sex

Maslow works which place transcendence at the top of the pyramid. Some great black leaders have modeled a spirit of going beyond self-actualization. Martin Luther King, Jr., and Howard Thurman are good examples. It must be stated, however, that the black religious experience has indeed made transcendence a goal for all. Transcendence was the critical necessity which enabled blacks to overcome the horrors of slavery. A spirit of transcendence still exists in the lives of many mature blacks who have had to find in church the liberation and peace that could not be found elsewhere. The tragedy among young blacks is that the economic climate in our country and a rise in materialism in society has made the achievement of the lower rungs of the hierarchy even more difficult. Education that is holistic in scope is critical to the continued development of the religious lives of black people. The goals of transcendence that have been a part of black religious life will rarely be achieved if churches do not find ways to address the pressing social issues of our times.

For this reason, a theology which deals with the black family must be holistic. The black family theologian does not have the luxury of setting aside an evening a week and solely devoting attention to small group discussions, one-to-one counseling, or even parent-child education. To take that approach alone is to attempt a white strategy, based on white cultural and economic attainments, upon a people who are facing much different cultural and economic issues.

Blacks have tended to avoid private and group counseling because even verbalization of certain psychological feeling level matters presupposes certain personal and societal *a priori* understandings which in black culture are not present. Skills development attempts through classroom experiences are often futile unless other matters are also being addressed. The black parent or child who might come to such sessions cannot hear cognitive material at the deepest core of his or her being if the primary problem being faced is one of physiology, self-esteem, or the need to be loved.

For this reason, the reality that the black family and the black church function as co-sufferers must be the point at which a church program to enrich the family begins. Such a program must begin at the point of understanding the depth of suffering which is, for America's slave descendants, still the most immediate problem being faced.

The offshoot of understanding this basic reality is that any effective family enrichment program for the black church must be both holistic and patient. Such a program must be holistic (the most important ingredient) because the enrichment that families need in order to deal with their suffering takes the church into areas of ministry which heretofore have been foreign. Any church that is attempting to deal with improving the plight of the black family must be strategizing ways to develop safe, sufficient housing, bringing pressure to bear on health care facilities for adequate treatment of the poor, insisting upon the best education available no matter what the income level of the various school districts, and seeking to develop marketable production centers where black folk can be empowered to control the means of production and distribute wealth equitably among the masses.

The preceding paragraph certainly points out why patience is the second most important ingredient of a black family-enrichment program. The development of the societal substructure in which blacks can experience the wholeness necessary for the ultimate development of a broad-based system of family stability will not come quickly. The point that must be stressed is that the plight of the black family is not just the result of some fault endemic to black people. The problems of the black family go into the very depth of the centuries of negative imagery, poverty, and oppression that have been perpetrated by the Western world upon African descendants.

This point must be driven home as much to middle-class blacks as to whites. There is a very troubling sound which has begun to move through black communities. It is the sound of middle-class blacks distancing themselves from the plight of the so-called underclass. It is a sound which is as right wing and reactionary as anything being voiced by the Moral Majority. It is not uncommon to hear blacks who have arrived berate underclass blacks as those who are too lazy to work or who only want to lay up and have sex and not take care of their responsibilities. Those blacks who verbalize those insensitivities are in some ways more of a problem than the bigots who originate such statements. They are more of a problem because invariably they are the ones everyone from Jerry Falwell to the electronic journalists highlight to dramatize the fact that blacks are not united in their criticism of this society's evils. The black pastors and black leaders who are interested in doing serious family enrichment must begin by rigorously discrediting anyone who betrays our struggle for freedom because he or she has become successful. Pastors must remind all such pretenders who say they have achieved the middle-class dream that the major difference between a middle-class white and a middle-class black is that a middle-class black is only one firing away from the ghetto. Statistics are beginning to show that the so-called underclass blacks are increasingly those who are not coming to the main-line black churches. Sadly, the frontline churches with the large memberships, the wonderful choirs, and the numerous clubs are impotent when dealing with the problems of gang violence, drug addiction, and so forth because people most affected by those problems are not of that ten percent who consider themselves regular church attenders.[8]

The dilemma that comes to the surface is, "If I cannot do everything, can I do anything?" At that point the individual pastor, Christian educator, or whoever begins the work of doing family enrichment is the key to the success of such a program. Blacks in America are not all at the poverty level. Even blacks who are poor range from some just this side of starvation to others who may just be seriously underemployed for their abilities. The developer of a program of family enrichment must be sensitive to the needs of the persons that are being worked with, and he or she must develop a number of programs flexible enough to deal with the awesome differences within the community.

What this means is that some blacks, although seriously impoverished, will still be able to verbalize relational and feeling matters well enough to need more educational experiences to enable their development. Still others, to be enriched as families, are first going to need houses, jobs, and education. The process of family enrichment for blacks must then be holistic because it must deal with the totality of the black plight. To deal with this totality, such an enrichment program must continually work to keep an equilibrium between the individual and the group. The error of so many white-oriented family enrichment programs is that they are almost entirely individualistic. They are based on an enlightment-type mode of thinking. Their bottom line is that each individual has the power to get himself or herself in shape if the right information is appropriated. Even those who develop a family systems approach often merely expand the individual to the individual's family system as that which, with the right information, is able to right itself. For black family enrichment, however, the extended family model holds the potential for maintaining the individual versus societal equilibrium without simply speaking of a nuclear family as if it were an individual. The extended family structure starts with the sanctity of each individual, understands that each individual has been primarily socialized by mother and father, but then by virtue of family extension sees self, mother, and father as related to others. The words "related to" are used intentionally because these words keep in focus the organic nature of society and in turn force us to see that society's problems and the individual's problems are not so easily separated, but are indeed related one to the other.

6

A Comprehensive Approach to Family Enrichment

The task in the development of this family enrichment program is to define strategies whereby the authentic identity of black people as persons made in the image of God can be recaptured. The establishing of authentic self-image is critical when one realizes that this area is where racism, since the Neoclassical period, has done its most insidious harm.

The family has been devastated by the relentless evils of those so-called sciences that have used scientific methodology to put forth boldly or imply stealthfully that inferiority is inherent to the black condition. These theories hold that either blacks are innately inferior, as natural selection would prove through black subservience to whites, or that blacks (if not genetically inferior) are at least culturally inferior as a result of slavery and colonialism. Either of these positions when reinforced by biblically conservative folk who hold to the Ham doctrine[1] somewhere in their psyche provides for the climate that makes majority persons hate and fear blacks.

In the best sense of sociobiological theory, majority people perceive the weakness of black people as a potential threat to the further development of the white race. Any allowance of cross-cultural fertilization (busing for instance) can only pull back whites. Whether it advances blacks is immaterial! Any permission of miscegenation has the potential for bastardizing the white race and infusing in its blood the same inferior genetic traits that have held down blacks.

A model for family enrichment that holds the image of God central to black development is critical because it first provides a way for black people to define self without the taints of racial prejudice which infest the television and all major publications. Secondly it provides an authentic family-oriented hermeneutic which exposes the satanic nature of the curse of Ham doctrine.

To be holistic, this family enrichment model must address the three most important areas faced by human beings. The first of these is the material. As Maslow has well stated, the higher levels of human achievement cannot be approached as long as persons have not had the basic necessities met. Second, at the psychological and the sociological levels persons need the experience of wholeness which comes about through a better understanding of who he or she is inside, and persons need the mutual support of improved relationships. Third, all of this must be internalized through the deeper values of salvation both for individuals and corporate structures through repentance and regeneration.

The most radical way to accomplish these goals is through a rethinking of the way Christian education is accomplished. The programs that are needed to provide support for the beleaguered black family are programs that are new and different for most black churches. Black churches historically have done their Christian education through Sunday church school and an occasional adult Bible class. That model is no longer effective. Sunday church school must be radically reshaped with curriculum either chosen or designed which first and foremost promotes an understanding of the self and the group as a family in which one has membership because one is made in God's image and is God's child. The basic teaching of the Bible should be accomplished through an explication of the texts so that biblical material can be understood in light of the core reality of what it means to be a member of God's family.

Adults need also to receive the same core presentation of an enhanced self-image, and this can be accomplished through adult educational experiences as well as through preaching the themes of human liberation. After ten years of preaching, I was astounded to hear a young woman in our congregation testify at a prayer meeting that she intended to organize parents in the community to protest the horrible public school system of Chester. She reported that she had been listening to the pastor's sermons all these years and realized that we have to take control and stop waiting for people to do things for us. This statement from a woman with no formalized theological training was as profound an expression of the theology of liberation as I have heard in any classroom.

In this same vein education cannot just be classroom experience. It must be balanced with learning that takes place experientially. As leader and parent, the pastor has the potential to effect tremendous learning through the organizing of persons around the specific goals and tasks. In turn, the pastor can also be co-learner because some of the education needed for the overcoming of the black plight will be that which the community sees as teams of pastors organize themselves to unify their churches for cooperative effort. According to Virginia Satir,

> "The family is the 'factory' where physically healthy, mentally alert, feeling, loving, playful, authentic, creative, productive human beings are made. In every family there are four basic forces which are at work; the self-worth of the members, communication among members, rules about how to feel and act, and the members' link to the society around them."[2]

Satir's remarks point clearly to the reality that the family must be understood in the light of the environment it faces.

The black family is facing a twentieth-century holocaust of economic and psychological deprivation which mandates a national strategy for addressing the problem. In an era of retrenchment for social programs and a spirit of benign neglect coming from government, the only hope for the development of a national strategy geared to the problem is through black churches.

The black church is built on the African concept of the extended family; so it is a natural place to do comprehensive family enrichment. Such an enrichment program has a two-pronged purpose. First, it addresses the needs of black families, and, second, by strengthening families it strengthens and buttresses the heart of the black church.

The strategy for achieving the goal of a national effort by churches to concentrate on family problems is founded upon a radical rethinking of Christian education. This virginal definition of Christian education requires a church's commitment to shape its entire witness around a family model. The ministry of the church would be based on educating an entire congregation to see its work as being both the work of a family and work to families. This work would be both cultus and mission. It would address the problems of black families both within the congregation and internationally with the ultimate theological goal being to reunify humankind and the original image of God. That image indeed is descriptive of the human community as God's family.

The practical expression of this approach would educate persons through preaching, teaching, and example that church finances and stewardship programs may have greater success when the congregation feels itself to be a family. The curriculum should be designed so that it not only informs persons as families, but also informs them of the importance of family. Social events within the church can be arranged to maximize the importance of family, and mission work can be effectively accomplished when it is thought of as the families within the church reaching out to each other and the church family reaching out to the families of the community and of the world.

This innovative approach to Christian education needs a four-pronged attack to elucidate its message to congregations. The first is through preaching. We mentioned earlier that this approach will not be implemented quickly. It calls for a fundamental rethinking for many of what constitutes the nature and mission of the church. The positive result of that thinking is that for black people the family as a way of conceiving church is a dominate archetype. The catalyst for bringing the archetype to consciousness must be the preacher. She or he must take leadership in modeling the concept of church family, and she or he must preach the ringing inspirational sermons of liberation;[3] that will direct parishioners to appreciate ministry with and to families as their first priority. There may be some blocks to this direction. For example, it will not be easy for churches to allow youngsters who are not parishioners but in trouble with the law to utilize church space for educational or social programs of rehabilitation. This block can be overcome by getting church persons to understand that, as church members, when they open their doors to others, they are drawing upon the adoptional concepts which have been a part of black tradition. The preacher can help them to understand this, but through a strong program of preaching and witnessing to these truths, she or he must be setting the stage for this type of action long before any such program is shaped.

Classroom educational experiences through Sunday church school lessons, adult Bible classes, and workshops are the second prong of the attack. Again, the concepts being taught are new; they need to be introduced to persons in nonthreatening ways so that they can be heard, not just reacted to. Careful thinking must be done on the part of persons with educational expertise within the congregation as to how best to maximize the classroom's potential.

Counseling is the third prong. Counseling encompasses the sphere of families within as well as outside the church. An effective counseling program is too big to be accomplished just by the pastor. Peer counseling teams may be formed as one way to increase participation. Where possible, professional assistance can be employed. One must always remember, however, that for black people one-to-one relationships are almost always the only effective way to do counseling. These relationships must form along lines that people feel are most comfortable. Sometimes people will talk to a deacon, member of a mothers' board, or advisor to a youth group. These same people will rarely discuss intimate problems with someone they view as professional. Peer counseling teams should then be recruited from within the church to reflect age, sex, and economic differences.

The fourth prong of the attack is community organizing. Much of what black families need to be effective is overall strengthening of their economic well-being. Strengthening economic well-being is critical to the success of a program for social change. In some ways, organizing persons to control their destinies is the most difficult of the four prongs. Community-based, people-powered organizations must be developed within churches as a way to reach out to the unchurched for the purposes of organizing communities to find major employers and industry for themselves, to improve education in public schools, and to renovate and restore run-down housing.

Turning the entire church program into a program of family enrichment takes the solution for the problem out of the realm

of a seminar or some series of lectures on the problem and
makes the goal of family enrichment the entire theological base
out of which the church understands its "cultus" and performs
its *diakonia* (mission).

The overall goals for the radicalized form of family theology
and education are the following:

1. To heighten self-image by recognizing that all persons are
created in the image of God.
2. To familiarize black Christians with materials and methods that enhance holistic family enrichment.
3. To develop skills which help persons to be better able to
cope with the problems of racism.
4. To understand the economic and political dimensions of
racism.
5. To develop skills that help families to improve relations
in spite of the hardships they face.
6. To establish family-based theology as a liberating power
which so models the biblical witness that it contains the potential to transform the world.
7. To develop in persons a biblical theological knowledge
which mandates their becoming agents of change.

Using Maslow's hierarchy of needs, let us now establish a
paradigm out of which this family-oriented program of Christian education might proceed. We must hasten to add that
Maslow's hierarchy is used as a way of structuring the paradigm. It is not being suggested that churches must do these
programs sequentially. Programs must be developed in which
education is addressing each of these issues simultaneously.
We must always remember that each family of the church is
going to be at a different place on the experiential time line.

Economic Development

Economics is the critical starting point for the healing of the
black families. A radicalized program of Christian education
can begin at this level by doing comprehensive community
organizing. This form of education operates in the following
ways:

1. It teaches through example that persons who have felt

themselves to be powerless really have more power than they suspect, therefore enhancing the understanding that we are not powerless for we are indeed made in the image of God.

2. Comprehensive community organizing provides persons with an opportunity to understand the gospel in light of much different political and social perspectives than those that had ever previously been raised.

3. It provides an opportunity for persons from various age groups and differing economic conditions to overcome these differences and be truly intergenerational, truly inclusive male and female, and truly classless, thereby modeling an essential understanding of the kingdom of God as Jesus articulated it in Luke, chapter 4.

The model that we have discussed as the touchstone for cooperative development of families and churches is that of co-suffering, adoptionists, and inclusive communities.

Ministry to black families must make the foundation of its holistic approach aggressive work in the area of economic development. To be healthy, every family needs steady income, quality housing, and access to effective educational institutions. Ministering to these areas certainly seems like an awesome task. The temptation of any busy pastor is to throw his or her hands up and say, "I just do not have the energy, the time, or the resources to perform this task." In response to that sentiment persons in the black church must continually remind one another that the proposals we are discussing are not luxuries but necessities. If time cannot be shifted from other responsibilities to concentrate on these areas, we are, in effect, sentencing our church's future to a slow and agonizing demise. If persons in need do not see an aggressive stance being taken by the church to bring about justice, they will turn to other sources to find solutions.

In this area pastors and leaders must abandon Lone Ranger approaches to ministry. Black churches will have to overcome tribal rivalries for the good of the race as a whole and cooperate fully. Ministers no longer have the luxury of assuaging our egos by competing for the finest care and the most prestigious parsonage. Bragging about the size of our budgets or the millions spent on our church renovations is counterproductive to

serious strategizing and the planning for comprehensive economic development. The watchword is cooperation. Pastors, lay
leaders, and churches must cooperate fully for the establishment of programs of economic development that will give black
families a chance. Dr. Johnnie Monroe, pastor of the Thomas
M. Thomas Presbyterian Church in Chester, Pennsylvania,
president of the Black Clergy of Chester, and former chairman
of the board of the Chester Opportunities Industrialization
Center, believes that churches should begin in doing economic
development. Churches should incessantly raise moral issues.
(One moral issue is the concept of redlining by banks, i.e., the
intentional denial of loans to persons living in certain areas is
immoral.) It is not the business of business to raise moral issues. In a capitalistic society a business has only one concern
and that is to run profitably. The church is the only institution
whose vested interests lie in the area of corporate morality.

To add to this point, there have been examples where, under
moral pressure, banks and investment firms have been brought
to see that investments in impoverished areas may not be the
economic disaster that some have foretold. Berean Savings and
Loan in Philadelphia, the oldest black-owned bank in America,
works very closely with the black churches of Philadelphia.
Through a cooperative effort of Berean and the black clergy of
Philadelphia, other banks were brought to see that Berean had
been investing for years with considerable financial profit in
the very areas that other banks had redlined. Out of this enforced morality through practical example, the Philadelphia
Mortgage Fund developed. It was a cooperative effort of black
churches, black investment firms, and white banks for the purpose of providing low-interest loans to minority people.

In addition to raising the moral issue, black churches cooperatively must establish partnership with private investors.
Often this must be done in spite of the local governments, which
usually give the assurance that all is being done that can pos-
sibly be done. Churches must never sit back and remain idle
simply because of this well-worn statement. Area representa-
tives, both state and local, and local chambers of commerce
should be contacted for leads. Advertisements for business may

also be placed in national and local business publications. Communications should then be made to these businesses directly. The watchword, again, is aggressiveness. Economic retrenchment during the Reagan presidency ought to have taught poor persons in this nation one sobering lesson, namely, if we do not do it for ourselves, no one will do it for us.

Short of this huge step, there are other areas of economic development where churches can bring moral pressure. One of these is to apply pressure on stores and businesses which practice charging higher prices in poor communities. This happens quite often at stores located near senior citizens' housing. Elderly family members could be greatly helped if churches would form watchdog teams to go about doing comparison shopping and, if necessary, organize boycotts against those businesses that are taking advantage of the elderly. Studies have also been done which show that prices in poor communities also rise at the time the government checks are issued. Capitalism is built on supply and demand, but such blatant manipulation is clearly immoral and cannot go unchallenged by churches who are interested in doing ministry to families.

If churches could pool resources, the possibility of churches starting their own businesses would develop. Clothing stores, food cooperatives, restaurants, even light manufacturing and high-tech industries, are all possibilities. Good suggestions can be gleaned from the current crop of books which give economic trends for the next several decades. Teams of young church members could form groups just to read such books and bring back suggestions of potential business opportunities. Utilizing the energy of young people on such a project would have as a side value the building of intergenerational community within churches.

One very successful example of a church-developed business is the Harvest Home Restaurant sponsored by the Bethany Baptist Church of Brooklyn, New York, pastored by Dr. William A. Jones. This restaurant, built totally from the contributions of church members, is able to serve many and employs a number of church members in its operation.

The work started by Dr. T. J. Jamieson, president of the National Baptist Convention U.S.A., Inc., is an attempt on the part of that convention to develop economic programs. This

network is certainly a worthwhile program for Baptist churches to explore. Other denominations may have similar national
strategies. Inquire about such programs through the various
denominational headquarters.

Where there are no existing programs, churches that share
a geographical affinity should consider adopting strategies
where one-tenth of each church's budget could be laid aside for
doing the work of economic development. This is actually a
missions approach that focuses on home problems. Many black
churches have for years raised thousands of dollars for overseas
missions but have left mission work at home in the hands of
government agencies. The new holocaust against poor people
brought about by President Reagan's domestic policies is an
indication that the work of missions at home is equally as
important as the work of missions overseas. With this tenth of
their budgets invested cooperatively, churches could generate
the capital necessary to begin doing serious economic development. Black families will never be stabilized if churches and
families do not find ways to address their shared economic
impoverishment. As extended families working together,
churches with some creativity can overcome the fact that few
black nuclear families in this country have access to enough
capital to do serious economic development.

Housing

At the Calvary Baptist Church in Chester, Pennsylvania, we
have formed a partnership with persons in the community and
with nearby Swarthmore College to address some of the problems facing black families. One of the worst problems is inadequate housing. Our observations have led us to see that
much of the powerlessness felt by blacks is because so many
own so little. Many live in a government housing project which
has "silly" laws that make it cheaper for two persons to live
together in an adulterous relationship than to marry. If they
enter into a legitimate marriage, the government increases
their rent by reducing their subsidies. A reality of the black
family's plight in America is that the government, through its
oppressive tactics, encourages illicit relationships and illegitimate births, then blames the victims for their victimization.

Another reality is that the average rent paid by blacks in

poor neighborhoods is way out of line for the amount of space received and the services provided. Through our research we discovered that a family which was paying $200 a month in rent and $150 in utilities could, even considering taxes, afford to buy a house somewhere in the eight- to ten-thousand-dollar range. Two church members with construction skills, Brother Walter Clark and Brother Leonard Dorsey, sat down with students Salem Schuckman and Dana Lyons from Swarthmore College, who had come to Chester looking for an inner-city education, and developed a strategy. With volunteer labor from Swarthmore students, church and community people, and the construction management of people like Brothers Clark and Dorsey, we could find houses with low or no back taxes, buy them, and completely rehabilitate them for between eight and ten thousand dollars. Construction work is not easy, and the project has not been without rough edges, but several persons have moved into houses and are now homeowners in a context which previously had caused them to see themselves as just victims. A complete description of the project appears in Appendix D.

The important point is that safe, sound, inexpensive housing is a critical need of black families in America. It is clear that government's indifference leads to the political system attempting to do very little. Churches must organize themselves and the communities they live in to see how critical a housing rehabilitation strategy is for a holistic family ministry.

Public Education

The state of public education in America is deplorable. Its severity throughout the nation is heightened by the problems of poor people. Violence within inner-city schools is on a shocking increase. Teachers feel threatened, good students are afraid, and parents feel powerless. The problems of education cannot go overlooked in any holistic family ministry. Families must be organized to face what certainly is one of the three or four greatest problems facing black America. Over fifty years ago W. E. B. Du Bois said that one of the greatest problems facing black Americans is miseducation, i.e., blacks are continually being geared up for services that are no longer marketable. The schools have a responsibility to speak to these needs, but schools have become woefully inadequate to face the task.

What strategies could potentially be of help? First, a cooperative effort could be established between the churches and the schools. A group could be organized within a church to act as the church's local chapter of the Parent-Teacher Association. These groups in the various churches could meet on a regular basis to strategize demands to be made and complaints to be lodged at the time of the regular P.T.A. meetings. These groups could also be the catalysts for local strategies aimed at systematically attending school board meetings and city council meetings, as well as monitoring local papers to make sure all governmental decisions are caught well before they are implemented if those decisions are dilatory to the progress of black families. Second, with the high instance of two-parent employment and one-parent families, most black families face the dilemma of their children getting out of school somewhere around 3 P.M. and most parents not getting home until 5, 6, or even 7 P.M. In this several-hour gap youngsters are the most susceptible to problems. Churches could fill this gap by opening their doors during this time and serving as drop-in centers. Many young people would just like a warm place to socialize where street pressures are not present. The church is an excellent place where the church extended family can fill a gap for the nuclear family. Activities could be planned, but by and large just a friendly, caring place to go is the greatest need. Supervision could be provided by retirees in the church family. Senior persons who are sensitive and caring could provide a real service by just being available to listen to youngsters, who during these hours may be experiencing some of their greatest social and psychological pains.

The education received by members of black families in public schools must be intentionally balanced and supplemented by a sound Christian education in the churches. As families we must encourage our churches to write their own Sunday church school and vacation Bible school literature so that it addresses the needs of our families. Creating effective literature can be done by individual churches simply developing supplemental exercises which get at the heart of each church family's uniqueness. It can also be groups of churches coming together with each church's needs in mind. Denominational resources may be of tremendous value at this point; however, such programs should be sensitive to the differences in age and the fact that all black churches have some wide disparities in economic, educational, and cultural backgrounds. In *Church Administration in the Black Perspective,* Samuel McKinney and Floyd Massey have produced a work which helps black folk better understand these important differences.[4]

Curriculum should be designed with special sensitivity to the unique needs of the elderly, the young, and the young adults.

We should know that in 1978 the Bureau of Census estimated that there were 2.8 million blacks aged 60 and older, or 11 percent of the total black population. In 1980, 800,000 blacks or 38.1 percent of the total black population, were below the poverty level. Aged blacks are nearly three times as likely to be poor as elderly whites. These statistics are exacerbated by the fact that another 310,000 blacks over 65 are marginally poor. These people have incomes which exceed the poverty level by only 25 percent. The sum total then is that 1.1 million blacks over 65 are either in poverty or close to the poverty line.

Black elderly persons rely very heavily on their Social Security checks as their primary income. For most blacks, Social Security is a kind of retirement plan. Black families, while doing the business of education, must keep clearly in mind that black elderly persons need continual assistance with financial management, monthly planning, and guidance through crises, such as death or prolonged illness. In a society where Social Security costs are continually being tossed about as a means of budget balancing, black families must incessantly use whatever lobbying power that churches can muster to insure Social Security's strength. Should it be decimated by the budget balancing axe, it would mean the literal starvation of hundreds of thousands of black elderly.

Housing for many black elderly is substandard. Many bought their homes forty or fifty years ago and have not had the extra income to keep their homes in shape. Educational events in churches should be sensitive to this. Through teaching and preaching, church families should be encouraged to create programs such as an adopt-a-grandparent program in which teams of younger adults might volunteer their time, perhaps an occasional Saturday, to take on chores like painting, grounds maintenance, and light fix-ups which elderly persons could rarely afford or be able to do on their own. Where black elderly families live in public housing, it must be stressed that these facilities are often substandard. The nation's government, the nation's largest landlord, is a slumlord. Most public housing is similar to the nation's worst ghettos. The awesome nature of this problem will not be easily solved, but the problem must be monitored and groups of church families must continually lobby for justice and for a fair share of the government's economic pie.

Earlier I mentioned the problems of health care for blacks in general. It must be remembered as programs are developed that often the problems of blacks in general—such as housing, health care, and crime—are merely intensified when one deals with senior citizens. Educational programs sensitive to the problems of black elderly persons should include the following: (1) Visitation teams of church family members should visit the elderly of the church on a regular basis to ascertain needs and just to help them feel that they are still an important part of the family. (2) Church families could provide an important service in the area of transportation. Because of medical problems many elderly cannot drive themselves, and public transportation is the scene of much crime. The church could establish helping relationships in which persons might escort the elderly to doctors' offices and clinics, on shopping trips, and so forth. (3) Meals on weekends and holidays are often a problem for the elderly. Church families again could provide a vital service if weekend meals could be taken to those in need.[5]

Young People

As with the elderly, the problems for blacks in general are exacerbated for young blacks. Crime among teenagers and young adults in this society has reached epidemic proportions. By the time most blacks reach their late twenties to early thirties the rate of crime that they commit greatly diminishes. Some of this decrease is due to the natural process of maturation and some of it due to the particularly troublesome enigma the adolescent years are for blacks. Everything said so far about self-image is heightened during adolescence. Adolescent blacks are made to believe that they are ugly because of their skin color and their hair, and that they are ignorant because they cannot attain score averages on level with their white counterparts on national testing.

In a study done by the Center for the Study of Social Policy were the following statistics. Forty seven percent of the black families with children under 18 are headed by women. Only 55 percent of black men over the age of 16 are employed today, whereas in 1974, 74 percent were employed. Families headed by women are nearly twice as likely to be poor as two-parent families. In addition to the men counted in the study who have no jobs, 20 percent of the men aged 20 to 40 could not be found by the Census Bureau, and are presumed to have no jobs or permanent residences. Black children are particularly affected by poverty. Black youths in 1981 were about three times more likely to be in poverty than their white counterparts.

The picture is bleak, but certain realities must be kept in mind as black church families attempt to educate folk and fight these problems. The study pointed out that the poverty of black youth is largely a result of 47.1 percent of all black families with children being female-headed, single-parent families. The poverty of female-headed homes is largely because not only is there just the one salary, but that salary is often lower than that received by the white female counterpart. The educational strategy must address general, important points. Black male desertion rates must be addressed. The church family context is the place where this must begin. Young men must be challenged to remain with and support families even though all the odds of racism in our society attempt to drive them away. Such a challenge can only be made credible, however, if these young men see that black church families are also battling hard on the economic front to bring job parity and dignity to the employment available for black males. Concurrent with this educational strategy, churches must preach and teach against the dominant consumerism in our world which makes us judge our wealth by the things in our possession rather than the quality and extent of our loving relationships and commitments. This is idealistic to be sure, but black families might teach the families of the world an ancient Christian principle, namely, that treasure ultimately must be stored in heaven.

The rage that young blacks feel is fanned by the materialism of our society which dangles "things" tantalizingly before persons but then slaps their wrists and says, "No, you're poor; you can't have them." A person with no hope of being the president of a bank may ultimately decide the next best thing is to rob the bank.

Women must also be encouraged to pursue the best-paying jobs. Black women coming out of high school and college are channeled by their environment to accept the lower-paying jobs of clerk typist, secretary, nurse's aide, and so forth. These jobs are dead-end positions. As stated earlier, the poverty of female-headed homes is largely due to there being one salary which is often lower than that received by the white female counterpart. Black females as well as black males must be encouraged to strive for upwardly mobile positions. Anyone who can be an effective nurse's aide can also be a nurse.

The striving for better positions also has an important catch. Blacks must learn to handle standard English. Black English has some important cultural roots, but as a ticket out of the ghetto standard English is essential. A few have climbed without a command of it, but as a rule in the corporate world, how one speaks, dresses, and conducts oneself are critical for career advancement.

Following are some specifics which church families might consider when developing educational programs for the young and young adults.

With the very young preadolescent the self-image problem must be addressed and self-worth must always be stressed. Young children must be encouraged to sing, to dance, to paint, to speak, and to write. Young blacks learn at an early age to fear communication. This is a vestige of the southern tradition of children being solidly disciplined for being too sassy. Young black parents are entirely too violent with their children. "Spare the rod and spoil the child," as it is often interpreted, is a myth. Young people need discipline, not violence. Discipline needs to be consistent and fair. Young children need to know where the boundaries are and have a consistent sense of what the penalty is for crossing those lines. Consistency in discipline will do what an occasional severe spanking can never do. It will modify children's behavior and it will not have the side effect of stunting their emotional growth.

With the adolescent, the image problem can again be the crucial test. A strategy must be developed and utilized so that adolescents can feel at home with themselves and with others. It must always be remembered that at this age young people really do not feel at home with themselves. Their bodies are changing. They feel awkward. They are not sure how to relate to parents. When these typical adolescent dynamics are multiplied by the problems of poverty, rage begins to build up within the youngster, and social problems start being acted out in the community.

Young adults who do enter into a committed partnering relationship will need much help with the ethical problems being faced. Bible studies centering on ethical issues are useful. Fellowship groups where people of this age can come together to do things are helpful. Basketball teams, bowling leagues, parties, and dances are all potentially sound strategies. With this age as with other ages, feelings of isolation are acute and encouragement to communicate with others honestly and openly is critical. Young couples also need instruction on partnering and parenting. These concepts can be taught from a black perspective, with a biblical base. Young black couples who find almost no help from the social science materials written by whites for whites will find great support in a program which draws them back to their church roots for authoritative statements and also celebrates their uniqueness as blacks.

Epilogue

A Call to Action

Throughout the nation there is developing a consciousness of the potential within the black church. The political campaign of the Reverend Jesse Jackson, which evidenced much more support than originally predicted, is an indication of the growing black consciousness.

The 1960s were a time of taking power as a slogan; the 1980s and 1990s will be times of taking power through controlling the means of production within our society. This will not be easy. Those who oppress and hold power will not yield that power easily. The black church must lead the way in bringing about our society's transformation. Black families are the key to this process.

I attended a Jewish seder recently and was impressed by the way in which the celebration of the Passover is for the Jew a family event and a religious event. Religion maximizes family values; family structure lends itself to religious development.

The family and religious nature of the Passover celebration provides an excellent model for understanding how family and church can work together.

For blacks in the Christian tradition two events—baptism and Communion— can maximize the place of the church in the life of the black family. In his book *Sacraments as God's Self Giving,* James F. White points out that Protestantism has tended to equate preaching with the prophetic, at the expense of understanding the liberating power of the sacraments.[1]

White's understanding of the sacraments as tools of liberation is very much in keeping with the spirit of this book's
attempt to ground freedom in the concept of the family. If the
black church is indeed a family, then it does need specific rituals of reiteration where religious values and family values
can be stressed.

These rituals, however, must be consistent with the call for
justice and freedom. They cannot be an opiate or a tranquilizer;
they must be a stimulator and mobilizer for action.

According to White, one of the purposes of the sacraments
is to center justice in the context of convenantal love. He says,
"The sacraments are intimately connected to justice since sacraments provide means of acting out relationships by enfleshing
them in visible forms." [2]

Because the sacraments speak at the level of the symbolic,
they have a much greater potential than the sermon to give
clear messages about family, justice, and freedom. Galatians
3:27-28 outlines very clearly the New Testament sense of equality: "For all of you who were baptized into Christ have clothed
yourselves with Christ. There is neither Jew nor Greek, there
is neither slave nor free man, there is neither male nor female;
for you are all one in Christ Jesus."

From this text we can see that Paul speaks of baptism as a
way to prevent the placing of persons into stereotypical groupings. Baptism is not always understood this way, but this is
precisely what the apostle was referring to. Baptism is in ac-
tuality a sacrament of equality. Through baptism, Christians
are made a part of a royal priesthood. The priesthood of all
believers is a hallmark for the Protestant faith. When this is
kept in mind, denying the ordination of women is ludicrous
simply because the rite of baptism has already insured them
a place in a sexless, classless society where all are God's priests.[3]

When the equalizing power of baptism is understood, its potential is a vehicle for uniting family and addressing equality
and justice issues is tremendous. Baptism symbolizes the wa-
tery death and the resurrection to this new life of equality; it
symbolizes the process of all of us, big or small sinner, passing
through the same water; it symbolizes our giving of our selves
to each other as Christ has given himself to us.

Baptism also has a critical place in developing a black family theology because minority families and poor families in general are more decimated by societal ills than majority or middle-class people. All the statistics that have been cited in this book point to the brokenness that is endemic to black families.

Black families increasingly experience the violence of spouse abuse, the horror of rape, the tragedy of alcoholism, and the unspeakable terror of violent mutilations and murders. The rite of baptism is important for its equalizing power because the church must drive home the fact that males, females, and children are equal partners in God's plan. Violence can only exist in a society where persons are not allowed full equality or not treated with mutual respect.

Black men and women must not take out the frustration and rage that they feel on weaker males, females, or children. When rage is exhibited toward the weaker members of our society, it shows forth hierarchial behavior based on a Western, post-Enlightenment concept of success. Hierarchical behavior based on pecking orders is not a biblical concept. It is a pagan concept. The Bible is clear that from the beginning God's image was intended to be an image of mutuality. Baptism reiterates the total mutuality of our human existence. It may come as a shock to some, but black pastors who rigidly oppose women in ministry are not only misunderstanding the spirit of Scripture in its entirety but also are unwittingly preaching for the kind of rigid societal heirarchy which allows for those on top to exercise abuse and violence upon "inferiors" such as women and children.

There are some specifics that churches can do to insure that these ordinances are utilized to the fullest for developing family and modeling justice. These concepts must be stressed because the theological life of the church family is ultimately the source out of which all other transforming action is born.

In baptism, the preacher can take the time while persons are being directed to the baptistry or standing in the baptistry to give some of the history and dramatize the message of liberation that is taking place. Families can take part in the service by escorting the initiate to the steps of the baptistry and then, depending on logistics, gather around the pool where they, both immediate and extended family, can see clearly what is taking place. After the service has taken place and the candidates are now back in their street clothes, the importance of their new lives within the community should be stressed and equal time be given to both deacons and deaconesses to address the candidates and help them feel their place in this new family relationship. A closing altar prayer after which all the members of the church might literally put their arms around the candidates and hug them could have great symbolic power. Immediately following the service, a time of fellowship in which each newly baptized person and their families are presented and called by name and given an opportunity to say who they are and how they have experienced the moment could again be very powerful.

The powerful symbolism of baptism as an equalizing ritual has the potential to say to families—whether or not one is from a one-parent family, is a single grandparent raising one's children's children or whether one has experienced violence and domestic abuse, that "We are all one in Christ Jesus."

Just as baptism initiates us into this new order, Communion acts as the symbol of our continuance in this role. Communion is the meal which gives us our spiritual vitamins sufficient for the strength needed to wage war against evil. In Communion we pledge continually our remembrance of God's giving of God's self to us. We also pledge our continued bond as a community of faith grounded in God. Our Communion meal is a foretaste of the hope that we look for in that better kingdom which God has promised to us. Communion ultimately models equality because it is served in the same way without respect to persons—rich, poor, male, female, young, or old. The theological principle that Communion really models most clearly is reconciliation. We receive the bread and wine as our statement of being reconciled with God and with each other.

The reconciliation aspect of Communion is important to a black family theology. Just as the equalizing nature of baptism is important to break down the rigid structures of dominance and submission, Communion is important as a way of getting people on an eye-to-eye level in order to share together with God. Only when the partnering dimensions of baptism are understood can Communion be understood as the rite which cements mutuality within our society.

Christ came to the first Communion meal armed with a towel.

This was the master's way of showing us the reconciling work which must be done as a part of pledging our mutuality. There can be no real partnering if the persons involved in our community do not come into the presence of God and each other on their knees and armed simply with a towel. In the early church the Communion elements were brought to the service by the people. The bread and wine that were offered were literally the works of the people. This is where our word "liturgy" comes from— *leitourgia,* the people's works.

Communion in the context of black family theology must be understood as the time of reconciliation. The bread and the wine shared mutually must be understood as the symbols of life from the earth, the work of our hands. The drive for human reconciliation can only take place when—like the bread—dominance and submission are broken and—like the grapes—selfish desire is crushed for the greater goals of citizenship in God's kingdom.

One of the ways that the goals of reconciliation can be attained in a family-based Communion is for the preacher and deacons to commune the sick and shut-in with as many family persons at the same time as possible. Deacons should be instructed in ways that the theology of reconciliation can be stressed in their presentations. The imagery of the breaking of the bread and the crushing of the grape can be emphasized as ways to understand our human need to crucify hierarchical structures if we are ever to be reconciled with each other and with God.

The same imagery can be used in the regular church service, but there should be as much instruction as possible through sermons, lectures, Bible studies, and so forth as to the fundamental way in which Communion is the heart of the family celebration of our Christian "passover" from death into life.

Actions, of course, do speak louder than words. The crucifying of hierarchical relationships must be modeled as well as spoken. Black churches must work to have women represented in the ranks of their preaching core as well as in the diaconate. This is not going to be an easy process, but it is a right process and the energy both in prayer and in work must be directed to that goal. Children must be involved in the process as full participants as well. If churches are creative, ways can be developed to allow young people to take part in the actual Communion. In the Jewish seder the youngest person asks the initial questions, which begins the process of the head of the family retelling the story of the Passover. A similar model could easily be employed in black churches. This would have the effect of involving families in the Communion but not offending the sensibilities of those who feel only ordained persons should actually do the serving.

The basis of this black family theology is the fundamental belief that being made in God's image is the root of our faith. The image of God is, as we have discussed, an image of pure mutuality. It is an image both of maleness and femaleness. It is an image which is in no way skewed by either age, race, or sex.

To experience authentic liberation, black people must begin the process by liberating themselves from the bondage of their own dominant/submissive patterns. History indicates that as a people blacks have always experienced a mutuality of pain and suffering. Black young and old, male and female have not been spared the harsh realities of homelessness, joblessness, and substandard education. In our theology of liberation, black churches and families must not allow the same oppression within our communities that we have experienced from without.

Within the community of shared suffering, we blacks must work with all the force of our being to make sure that the rage which results from our suffering ceases to be turned upon ourselves in destructive ways. Rape, child molestation, battered spouses, "black-on-black" crime are all the sorry results of the suffering shared within the community. Churches must find ways to turn that negative of shared suffering into a positive. Historically, this was done through the mutual aid societies of our churches. Long before the government was involved in welfare, black churches were feeding the hungry. The feeding of the hungry in today's world is much more complex. Churches, as I have pointed out, do need to address these problems through food programs, housing rehabilitation, community job banks, and other economic development programs. Churches must also attempt to address the theological issues involved in suffering within our communities. Some of the rage that produces violent behavior comes about because persons feel frustrated and abandoned. A black family theology that addresses the problems of shared suffering must also understand that the church's primary job is to help persons comprehend the theological principles which focus on the problems of suffering. Every black church in America needs to work toward a staff of clergy and deacons who are well versed in the issues of theodicy and able to deal with rage. No people in America are more acquainted with the problems of Job than are black people. Yet our churches have rarely had a comprehensive approach to equip church folk to understand the biblical and theological roots of suffering.

Black family theology needs also to address the issues of inclusion in order to mobilize action in churches. Black people do not have time to play the male/female sexist games. Black women historically have shared equally in black suffering; they must now share equally in black leadership. Churches must begin developing classes, holding workshops, and generally raising the consciousness of our people on this critical issue. Our push for liberation is weakened if our best and brightest female leadership is continually having to face the divided loyalties of being both black and female. Our sisters can be co-opted into some feminist movements which are totally insensitive and racist simply because they are not getting the respect and total mutuality that they deserve from the black community. We as a people can never muster the strength to fight for our total liberation as long as we are allowing ourselves to be split by questions of male dominance and female submission. We must remember that in the history of our struggle to be free, no less a leader than Frederick Douglass was very strongly in favor of female equality even to the point of sacrificing some of his own credibility with black folk to support that which he knew was right. It is true that he was abandoned by the very white feminists that he sacrificed to support, but again, right must take precedence. What Douglass did in supporting equality of the sexes was right. To be authentic, a black family theology must also keep the issues of inclusion very much in the forefront of people's thinking.

Finally, we have mentioned that the black church historically was an adoptionist community. We must develop strategies to maximize the potential of this ancient concept.

Recently a young Swarthmore College student who came to work on our project in Chester, Pennsylvania, asked if I knew of any family in the city that he might stay with while he did his work. I mentioned his desire to my congregation and was surprised at the number of people who came forward saying that they would be willing to take him in. Even though he is white, he found a home with the Harris family of our church because of this deep and ancient concept that we are an adoptionist society.

When I was in college, I met a young Puerto Rican man who subsequently became my dearest friend. When he began experiencing personal problems, he simply moved in with us. I do not remember any long substantive conversations taking place with my parents about his coming in. When the need was established, it just became clear that it was right for him to live with us until he got himself straightened out. He never did get straightened out and eventually died of a brain hemorrhage which was the result, we are convinced, of a beating he received from local police when he was apprehended on suspicion of robbery. The fact remains that he essentially became family. We grieved when he died, just as we would have over blood kin.

This adoptionism is a powerful force in the black community. In Harlem it was the spirit of the extended family, out of which the famous rent parties of the Depression era emerged. It is the spirit that makes all black Americans feel that Martin Luther King is our son, father, or brother. We must mobilize this force for even greater good. Big Brother and Big Sister programs are critically needed in our community as well as Adopt-A-Grandparent programs.

Families of churches will need to find the strength to rise to the occasion and share our resources with others in need if we are ever to be free. One of the reasons why the Greek concepts of idealized beauty are so foreign to black people is that we are not a sight-oriented, but a hearing-oriented people. Persons in need do look apalling. They often look repulsive. The sight metaphor is not what the adoptionist concept of black family theology must rest on. This adoptionist concept must rest on hearing, not on seeing.[4] The cries of the disenfranchised, unlike the sight of them, are all the same. Those cries strike the higher chord of human compassion. It is not the sight metaphor but the hearing metaphor that we must turn to as a basis for this approach. A key statement of Jewish religion begins, "Hear O Israel the Lord thy God is one." [5]

The culmination of my work rests with the realization that much of what is needed is a maximizing of the black church's ability to educate its people comprehensively, for the theological issues of inclusion and the breakdown of hierarchical thinking are really at the heart of what is needed to change society.

Christian education must become family theological education if it is to have a chance to tackle the problems faced by black people. Included in the appendix of this book is a sample curriculum which can be used as a starter. I must hasten to add that this curriculum is only one example. It is only a small piece of an attempt to examine the issues of self-image from a partnering, parenting perspective. The black church world is in need of many other diverse curricular offerings that will come to grips with the issues that have been raised throughout this book but focused upon specifically in chapter 6. In the design of these curricula we must always be mindful that a basic assumption of black family theology as here outlined is that education changes lives. Unless our approaches to the task of educating black people seriously come to grips with the breadth of problems facing our communities, we will not have educated and we certainly will not have taken seriously the deep roots of an authentic, practical theology of liberation.

Appendix A

Practical System Considerations to Keep the Elderly from Being Treated as Nonpersons

"How do you think it feels to sit in a restaurant with your son and have a waitress ask him: 'How does your father like his eggs?'"

The following systems are involved in the practicality of helping the aged.

Information and Referral Services—Many older people and their families do not know where to turn when they need help, and in most cities there is no central agency that gives them the information they need.

Home Health Services—Visiting nurses, physicians' assistants, and trained health aids are available for older people who cannot easily get to a clinic, hospital, or doctor's office or who need the occasional attention of a health professional in their lonely lives.

Nutrition Services—Meals On Wheels delivers food to the homes of the aged. Hot meals are served at schools or senior citizen centers. Food stamps and supermarket discounts may be helpful to those who get inadequate nutrition because they cannot afford better meals or because they are too ill, too disinterested, or too confused to prepare good meals.

Transportation Services—Dial-a-bus, volunteer drivers, and reduced fares are available in many areas for the millions of elderly who cannot use ordinary public transportation because it is too expensive, too far away, or not designed for persons with the infirmities of old age.

Communication Services—Television, radio, books, newspapers, and magazines can help to reduce isolation and provide entertainment. Telephones also reduce isolation and provide a way to signal for help in times of emergency. However, six million older citizens cannot afford these services.

Legal Services—At low or no cost, there are legal services to help the many older people who are victims of "ageism," who are easy prey to con games and other frauds, or who are taken advantage of by unscrupulous landlords, business people, and greedy relatives.

Housing—Appropriate housing for the aged, i.e., housing that is safe, comfortable, clean, and accessible to shopping, transportation, recreation, and medical care, is still relatively rare.

Intergenerational Aid—Many college students and high school students are now helping the aged. Intergenerational programs hold much potential for constructive work for the elderly. Intergenerational work builds a family feeling among persons and allows the elderly to contribute their wisdom and nurture to the young people whom they encounter.

Appendix B

Developing a Black Family Enrichment Curriculum

In this following section is a sample curriculum to be used with young adults, either couples or singles between the ages of eighteen and forty. The curriculum is designed to work toward the goal of total humanization. It rigorously attempts to avoid what Freire in *Pedagogy of the Oppressed* calls "a banking concept." To Freire, this concept is typified by:

a. the teacher teaches; the students are taught
b. the teacher knows everything; the students know nothing
c. the teacher thinks, and the students are thought about
d. the teacher talks, and the students listen meekly
e. the teacher disciplines, and the students are disciplined
f. the teacher chooses, and the students comply
g. the teacher acts, and the students have the illusion.[1]

The Theoretical Basis for the Curriculum

The theoretical design of the curriculum was based on the following four goals:

1. To heighten self-image by recognizing that all persons are created in the "image of God"
2. To familiarize black Christians with materials and methods that enhance family enrichment
3. To develop skills that enhance family relationships
4. To heighten the awareness of black Christians to the particular problems that face the black family in America.

The lesson plan objectives designed to achieve these goals are consistent with the sentiment of Martha Leypoldt in *Learning Is Change.* She writes:

> A person involved in experiential education contemplates and reflects on what the activity means to his life. This kind of education is "real" because the learner is involved and the learning which results is his. He learns by reflecting, he learns by doing, he learns by being.[2]

The curriculum was developed with this model in mind. There were spaces provided for the class to reflect on their own experiences as those experiences relate to the material. There were exercises designed for skills development. There was open encouragement for the class members to be a part of the "process" of learning.[3]

Each lesson of the unit was designed with each specific objective stated in keeping with the sentiment of Ralph W. Tyler by identifying both the behavior to be developed and the context in which the newly learned behavior is to operate.[4]

This approach attempts to teach students processes or skills they need or will need to guide their lives and successfully deal with issues of "identity power and correctness." Values clarification is one such approach, emphasizing the process of prizing, choosing, and acting. Human relations training (in many forms, including communication exercises, Parent Effectiveness Training, encounter groups, and so forth) is another example, teaching the processes of listening, giving and receiving feedback, handling conflict, and other skills. Achievement motivation is another process approach emphasizing goal setting, moderate risk taking, and achievement planning.[5]

The overall family enrichment guidelines set down by Virginia Satir in *Peoplemaking* serve as the basic family enrichment theory:

> In my years as a family therapist, I have found that four aspects of family life keep popping up in the troubled families who come to me for help. They are the feelings and ideas one has about himself which I call self-worth. The way people work out to make meaning with one another, which I call communication, the rules people use for how they should feel and act, which eventually develop into what I call the family system; and the way people relate to other people and institutions outside the family, which I call the link to society.[6]

The ideas of self-worth and self-image are critical problems for black Americans. This curriculum deals with this particular area by familiarizing class members with exactly what it means to be a black American and how that wonderful uniqueness is enhanced when, through the introduction of the biblical element, blacks are able to see themselves as individuals made in the image of God.

Each session is designed to show clear communication as an important process in skills development. Klaus Krippendorf, writing on "Human Communication in Systems Perspective," points out that an "act of communion" [7] will answer the following questions: "who, says what, in which channel, to whom, with what effect?" [8] He goes on to say

> The scientific study of the process of communications tends to concentrate upon one or another of these questions. Scholars who study the "who," the communicator, look into the factors that initiate and guide the act of communication. . .Specialists who focus upon the "says what" engage in content analysis.[9]

It is the "who" and the "says what" that concern this series of sessions, for those concepts lead to clearer communication. The "who" (the individual) brings to communication the following, according to Satir: "He brings his body. . .He brings his values . . . He brings his expectations. . .He brings his sense organs . . . He brings his ability to talk . . . He brings his brain."[10]

The "who" as actor "says what" when he is in dialogue with another. In the dialogical process, the various pieces (body, brain, and so forth) that each person brings to the communication (dialogue) are acting upon the receiver as he is in receipt of messages from the sender and "vice versa." Communication, then, is words, feelings, attitudes transmitted and words, feelings, and attitudes received. Often, to be effective, communication must do exactly what Fritz Perls outlines as a goal of this therapy "to shift the 'inner conflict' between impulses and the counter-attacking resistance, into an open, aware conflict."[11]

A goal concerning communication skills development, when relating to black people, also has to take the following into account:

> Perhaps few people use vocal communication in as many and varied ways as the Afro-Americans, and the research that has been done, including my own writings, has scarcely unearthed the link-

ages and networks responsible for the significance of the spoken word in black America. A rich oral tradition, augmented by lyrical aspects emerging from the slavery experience, contributes to the impact of the word. Saying something and doing something are part of the same event, and it is this marriage of word and action which remains to be fully understood.[12]

The communication exercises are designed to dispel the myth that communication is primarily spoken communication. They are designed to show that communication is spoken communication and unspoken communication. Lederer and Jackson develop that idea when they say, "Everything which a person does in relation to another is some kind of message. There is no not communicating. Even silence is communication." [13]

Satir's "family system" idea is developed by the concepts of partnering and parenting and is coupled with the "link to society" through the "self awareness" aspect of the image of God; through the communication process, which is strengthened by positive self-awareness; and through familiarization with materials that can be helpful in understanding the family system concept.

The special design of family therapy for black Americans is dealt with as part of the theme for each lesson. The biblical perspective is also handled in this way. Each lesson is also designed with the times of each segment specifically planned (within the overall framework of one and one-half hours).

The various formats, taken from Martha Leypoldt's *40 Ways to Teach in Groups,* are lecture, role playing, brainstorming, work groups, discussion.[14]

The Design of This Family Enrichment Curriculum

The black church in America is still the primary unit in the black community where black people come together in mass and share the pains and problems of their human experiences. The curriculum is designed to be a tangible learning experience for black Christians, presented in local black churches, where individuality, personhood, partnering, and parenting can all be approached from both a biblical and a historical perspective.

The program is designed specifically for individuals or couples in the eighteen to forty age range who are either married, formerly married, or contemplating marriage, and who want to know themselves and the process of relating in a deeper, more qualitative way. The primary purposes of this curriculum are (1) to present family enrichment as a means of enhancing an understanding of one's createdness (in the image of God); (2) to increase black self-awareness through familiarization with materials and resources pertaining to black history and family enrichment; (3) to sensitize blacks to various potential family problems; and (4) to develop the skills that can aid the family when it is facing problems.

The program, or curriculum, consists of six sessions. The first session centers on individuality, enabling persons to see themselves from a black perspective as participants in the image of God. The second session introduces the importance of quality male-female relationships and the impact on individuality, personhood, and the image of God concept. The third session further develops the need for persons to recognize maleness and femaleness as a part of the image of God. The fourth session deals specifically with male-female interaction in partnering. The fifth session shows how partnering, in the sense of its relationship to the image of God, is the basis for persons becoming parents. The sixth session focuses on the whole notion of personhood and deals with children as persons.

Let me say right off that these sessions are meant to serve as one example of family enrichment curriculum. Readers are encouraged to look at their own situations for ways to develop material to suit their circumstances.

Let us now look at each session in more detail.

Session 1: *Personhood and Individuality*

In light of the massive problems (economic, cultural, and social) that face black Americans, being familiar with the divine ideal of being made in the image of God is critical if the positive aspects of selfhood, sexuality, responsibility, and personal growth are to be achieved. Frank Stagg says,

> Man finds this true existence in the polarity of solitude and solidarity, in individuality and community. As an individual he has an identity never to be confused with another. As a person he is necessarily in a bundle with God and his fellowman. Individuality is that which distinguishes a man from God and from other men and gives him identity and uniqueness. It cries out against every kind of stereotyping, whether racial, class, caste, sexual, age group, or some other kind. Personhood is that which vitally relates him to God and other persons. Man is not an island, for no man lives or

dies unto himself (Romans 14:7). Neither is man a part of a machine or a spark ultimately to be reabsorbed into a cosmic flame (stoicism). If man is to be truly man, he cannot escape the tension of this polarity. That he finds his true being in this polarity is the perspective of Scripture throughout.[15]

Self-image is a real problem for many black Americans; spending centuries being considered and treated as property rather than persons has had a dramatic effect on the emotional and spiritual well-being of many. To know that blackness does not separate persons from the image of God is an important step in the development of healthy self-image, and healthy self-image is critical to healthy relationships.

Objective of Session 1

The major objective for this session is for the class members to understand and communicate that being created in the image of God applies to all people and gives an added dimension to human sexuality, responsibility, and growth. The major concept to be learned is the ability to communicate clearly exactly what it means to be created in the image of God.

Lesson Plan

Scripture Text—Genesis 1:26-27, RSV (This same text is the basis of all sessions.)

Then God said, "Let us make man in our image, after our likeness; and let them have dominion over the fish of the sea, and over the birds of the air, and over the cattle and over all the earth, and over every creeping thing that creeps upon the earth." So God created man in his own image, in the image of God he created him; male and female he created them.

Major Concept to Be Learned

An appreciation for the fact that being created in the image of God applies to all people; and that unique createdness gives to black people an added dimension in sexuality, responsibility, and growth.

Methods

Lecture, role play, discussion.

Procedure

1. To set the context, give brief introductory remarks on problems of black family life.
   a. According to the Study of Social Policy, 47 percent of black families are single-parent and female-headed. Families headed by women are nearly twice as likely to be poor as two-parent families. In 1981, the median income for blacks was only 56 percent of that for whites. Forty-seven percent of blacks with four years of college earned $20,000-$40,000 a year. The same percentage of whites with high school education earned salaries in the same range. Black youths are about three times as likely to live in poverty as their white counterparts.[16]

2. Lecture
   a. The statistics indicate that blacks have little to make them proud.
   b. The fact that blacks share in the image of God is a source of pride and a builder of positive self-image.
   c. Genesis 1:26-27 has been translated and interpreted in many different ways. Farrar in *History of Biblical Interpretation* suggests that there are several major epochs of biblical interpretations:[17]
      Rabbinic Interpretation
      Alexandrian Interpretation
      Patristic Interpretation
      Scholastic Interpretation
      Reformation Interpretation
      Protestant Scholastic Interpretation
      Seventeenth Century Reformed Interpretation
      Modern Interpretation
   d. Some of the fallacies produced by these schools of interpretation are: the spirit is godly, the flesh is evil; sex is not a part of the image of God; women are inferior to men.
   e. Black people must be very careful not to fall into these fallacies.
   f. Black people can overcome racist attitudes when they affirm themselves as a part of the true image of God.

3. Have the class draw on paper graphs of the human body.

    a. Instruct the class to write on the graphs words that describe how they see God. Allow time for completion.

    b. Discuss the graphs. (Use a chalkboard or newsprint for brainstorming or listing the descriptive words arrived at earlier, if it is helpful.)

4. Give the following quote from James Olthuis's *I Pledge You My Troth:* "Man cannot be defined without woman, woman cannot be defined without man."[18]

    a. Show that in the Fall man and woman made the choice to disobey.

    b. Show that because of the Fall, intimacy is now seen as a curse, not a blessing.

    c. Show that sin caused Adam and Eve to search for a scapegoat, changing their relationship from helping and needing each other to denying and hindering each other.

5. Read Exodus 3:11; "But Moses said to God, 'Who am I that I should bring the sons of Israel out of Egypt?'"

6. Discuss this passage and the quote from Olthuis in light of human responsibility.

7. Role-play two skits. Two volunteers for each one are needed.

    a. A girl tries to tell her boyfriend that she is pregnant.

    b. A husband tries to tell his wife that he has been unfaithful.

8. Discussion

    a. Ask individuals how the development of positive self-image and the acceptance of responsibility lead to growth.

    b. What things enhance personal growth? What things hamper it?

9. Assignment: Hand out graph from Appendix C. Have class members draw themselves as they see themselves on the graph and bring the graphs to the next session.

10. Review. Restate the following.

    a. Persons are created in the image of God

    b. Persons are created male and female.

    c. Persons are created to be responsible.

    d. Responsibility leads to growth.

11. Evaluation: hand out evaluation questions (Evaluation 1) from Appendix C. Let class fill them out.

12. Collect evaluations, and dismiss the class.

Materials used: Books—James Olthuis, *I Pledge You My Troth;* Frederick Farrar, *History of Biblical Interpretation; New York Times*; and the Revised Standard Version of the Bible. (Except for the RSV, bibliographical information on materials cited in this section of each session can be found either in the "Notes" of Appendix B or the other "References for Appendix B," which follow the Notes.)

Session 2: *The Meaning of Personhood*

Frank Stagg says,

> Man is made to become, but he cannot become through himself alone. He cannot so transcend himself as to be able to lift himself up by his own bootstraps (Romans 7:7-25). He can become only in response to God who addresses him, and calls to him from without (Romans 8). When man becomes an authentic human being, it is the result of God's own creative work, calling men to an existence which moves in the direction of an essence which is from God (1 Corinthians 15:10; Galatians 2:20; Ephesians 2:10).[19]

Persons find out who they are by being in relationship with one another and with God. Black people have traditions and customs that are precious to them, and some of these go back to experiences of western Africa (even before forced slavery). Those customs do not hamper but enhance and give meaning to individual selfhood, primarily because societal customs are shared experiences. Correcting negative self-image is a basic step toward the strengthening of relationships. Virginia Satir describes positive self-image as "high pot" and says,

> Integrity, honesty, responsibility, compassion, and love all flow easily from the person whose pot is high. He feels that he matters, that the world is a better place because he is here. He has faith in his own competence. He is able to ask others for help, but he believes he can make his own decisions and is his own best resource. Appreciating his own worth, he is ready to see and respect the worth of others. He radiates trust and hope. He doesn't have rules against anything he feels. He accepts all of himself as human.[20]

Objective of Session 2

The objective of Session 2 is to demonstrate that people become persons when they (people) are in relationship with one another. Individuals should be able, upon completion of this session, to communicate clearly how the quality of relationships between males and females develops individuals into persons (in the image of God) and enhances self-image.

Lesson Plan

Major Concept to Be Learned

The clear communication of the ways in which quality male-female relationships develop individuals into persons.

Methods

Lecture, discussion, brainstorming.

Procedure

1. Lecture
   a. Family life in western Africa was a strong system for the communication of moral ideals and cultural values.
   b. Fathers were responsible for moral behavior.
      Fathers taught respect.
      Fathers taught obedience.
      Fathers taught deference.
   c. Fathers in their teachings were very strong on mutuality between parents and children. An Ashanti saying states: "A father's only method for obtaining obedience is love."
   d. Mothers tended to hold a very "saintly" position in western Africa.
      Mothers were responsible for the socialization of children.
      Mothers were considered the hub or heart of tribal society. Father was the head, but mother was the heart.
   e. Mothers were the quintessential role models to the female children and the closest confidantes of the male children.
   f. Grandparents, uncles, aunts, and cousins all formed the extended family.

    g. The quality of relationships in western Africa was based on:
The uniqueness of male-female sexuality;
Pure, non-stratified mutuality;
Spiritual as well as physical interaction.
The extended family is not only comprised of relationships with grandparents, aunts, and uncles, and so on; it is also comprised of relationships with both the unborn and the dead. (*Journal of Ethnic Studies,* vol. 4, no. 2, p. 152.)

    h. "Dominion over" was really dominion with, as all family members were mutually responsible for the well-being of the group.

2. Have the class reread Genesis 1:26-27 and then ask, "What does it mean to 'have dominion over'?"

    a. Spend some time brainstorming and recording responses on the board or newsprint.

    b. The instructor should lead the class in discussion to see how crucial the idea of responsibility is to the notion "have dominion over."

3. Have the class read Exodus 3:11 (review).

    a. The instructor should point out how responsibility is a part of this passage.

    b. For Moses, acceptance of responsibility was an important step toward his own growth.

4. Have the class read Ephesians 5:21 and answer the question "What is meant by mutual subjection?"

    a. Allow time for discussion.

    b. Lead the class to see that human sexuality:
      1) is a gift from God;
      2) is edifying when it is understood as mutuality.

    c. Refer to mutuality in western Africa as a basic principle of male-female relationships.

5. Establish the fact that the image of God is stated clearly as an image of humankind as male and female.

    a. Refer to Genesis 1:26-27 and establish that:
      1) true intimacy comes when men and women live according to the interrelatedness established in Genesis 1:26-27;
      2) true interpersonal intimacy enhances self-image.

    b. Refer to the intimacy which the quality of relationships in western Africa develops.

6. Ask the question "How does self-image affect our relationships?"
    a. Encourage the class to see that:
      1. healthy self-image is a problem for black people;
      2. healthy self-image helps healthy relationships to remain strong.

7. Review the basic principles.
    a. Dominion in relationships is a reflection of the image of God.
    b. Dominion and subjection are the basis for male-female interrelatedness.
    c. Male-female interrelatedness is a basic principle of the image of God.

8. Pass out the evaluation sheets (Evaluation 1, Appendix C). Allow time for the class to answer.

9. Collect the evaluation sheets and dismiss the class.

Materials used: Books—James Olthuis, *I Pledge You My Troth;* Lerone Bennett, Jr., *Before the Mayflower: A History of Black America;* Virginia Satir, *Peoplemaking.* Journals—*The Journal of Ethnic Studies.* A sketch of the human body.

Session 3: *Persons and Partnering*

In light of the image of God, maleness and femaleness must be recognized as a basic principle in the whole understanding of a systems concept of male-female interrelatedness. Lederer and Jackson make the following statement in *Mirages of Marriage:*

> The principles of the systems concept has been understood for a long time. A Babylonian astronomer said "Heaven is more than stars alone. It is the stars and their movements." According to the systems concept the whole is more than the sum of its parts.[21]

This session is designed to teach, through the systems concept, an understanding of both the responsibilities and the growth germane to partnering. The session seeks (1) to move the class toward seeing that marital relationships involve not just coequal selves, but co-dependent and co-responsible selves;

and (2) to demonstrate that these selves are created in the image of God.

Objective of Session 3

To be able to state clearly how people become effective persons through a systems understanding of interrelatedness. By the end of the session, class members will be able to state clearly the importance of male-female interaction for strong family relationships.

Lesson Plan

Major Concept to Be Learned

To be able to clearly state how people become more effective persons through a systems understanding of interrelatedness.

Methods

Brainstorming, discussion, role play.

Procedure

1. The instructor draws on the chalkboard two columns, one for the attributes of God and one for the attributes of self. Let the class brainstorm items to fill both columns.

2. Have the class read Mark 10:2-8 (RSV), "And Pharisees came up and in order to test him asked, 'Is it lawful for a man to divorce his wife?' He answered them, 'What did Moses command you?' They said, 'Moses allowed a man to write a certificate of divorce, and to put her away.' But Jesus said to them, 'For your hardness of heart he wrote you this commandment. But from the beginning of creation God made them male and female. For this reason a man shall leave his father and mother and be joined to his wife and the two shall become one flesh.'"

3. Raise the question "How does what we understand about God and what we understand about self affect our human sexuality?"

    a. Discuss the question. (During this discussion the instructor should review the last session on individuality and personhood. It should be demonstrated that some of the positive aspects of God [raise these if they have not been raised], such as love, caring, and giving, cannot be experienced by individuals in isolation. They can only be experienced by persons through relationships.)

    b. Direct the class to see love, trust, and commitment, as by-products of human interrelatedness.

4. The instructor should read the following quote from Lederer and Jackson, *Mirages of Marriage,* p. 87. "The principle of the systems concept has been understood for a long time. A Babylonian astronomer said, 'Heaven is more than the stars alone. It is the stars and their movements.' According to the systems concept, the whole is more than the sum of its parts."

    a. Explain the systems concept in basic language (use the example of the ingredients of a cake and the final product they make).

    b. Discuss the question "How is your family a system?" (Through the discussion the instructor should ascertain how well the concept is being absorbed. Time may be adjusted to insure that the concept of systems is grasped as this is so critical to this lesson.)

5. Perform the role play (adapted from Virginia Satir, *Peoplemaking,* p. 80) in Appendix C.

6. Discuss the role play from these following aspects:
    a. How did you (the individual) feel about the role play?
    b. What did you learn from the role play?
    c. What did you not like about it?
    d. What did the role play say to you about relationships?

7. Encourage the class to copy the columns of attributes and to reflect on them further in light of the insights gained from this lesson.

8. Review: people become persons through interrelatedness; relationships are systems; systems need clear communication; communication enhances love, trust, and acceptance; love, trust, and acceptance are all responsibilities based on being created in the image of God (i.e.,

they are given by God to humankind as dominion over creation).

9. Hand out evaluation sheets (Evaluation 1) from Appendix C.

10. Collect evaluation sheets. Dismiss the class.

Materials used: Books—Lederer and Jackson, *Mirages of Marriage*; Virginia Satir, *Peoplemaking*.

Session 4: *The Problems of Partnering*

For the black American, there are unique problems related to the question of marriage. This session is designed to examine those problems and to familiarize people with materials that can be helpful when these problems need to be faced.

It is often assumed, particularly by liberal intellectuals and sometimes by social scientists and social workers, that what is required of Negro families in our society is essentially the same as what is required of white families. According to this view, it is not the demands made on the family, but the ability of the family to meet these demands which distinguishes Negro family life. If, however, the Negro people are viewed as an ethnic subsociety, it can be appreciated that while there are basic similarities in the requirements for Negro families, there are peculiar requirements which grow out of three factors: (a) the peculiar historical development, (b) the caste-like qualities in the American stratification system which relegates all Negroes to inferior status, and (c) the social class and economic systems which keep most Negroes in the lower social class."[22]

Objective of Session 4

This session seeks to demonstrate that in light of the special problems that face the black family, the decision to marry must be made carefully and in keeping with the whole scriptural understanding of male-female interrelatedness. By the conclusion of the class, class members should have a clear understanding of what the problems are that face black partners.

Lesson Plan

Major Concept to Be Learned

To develop a clear understanding of the problems that face black partners.

Methods
Role play, brainstorming, discussion, lecture.

Procedure

1. Have the class read aloud Ephesians 5:21-24.
2. Ask the question "Why do people get married?"
   a. Write the responses on the board or newsprint.
   b. Discuss the responses.
3. Write on the board or newsprint the seven false assumptions of marriage, according to Lederer and Jackson, pp. 41-84.
   a. People marry because they love each other.
   b. Most married people love each other.
   c. Love is necessary for a satisfactory marriage.
   d. There are inherent behavioral and attitudinal differences between females and males, and these differences cause most marital troubles.
   e. The advent of children automatically improves a potentially difficult or an unfulfilled marriage.
   f. Loneliness will be cured by marriage.
   g. If you tell your spouse to go to hell, you have a poor marriage.
   Discuss these false assumptions one by one, restating them in question form (do people marry because they love each other?).
4. Give a brief lecture on marriage customs of western Africa.
   a. Point out that:
      1) After marriage, a western African couple almost always moved in with the family of the bride and rarely with the family of the groom;
      2) Neolocal family systems were discouraged for economic reasons, but more importantly for psychological reasons. The extended family was considered the best tool for personal development;
      3) Sexuality was encouraged as a positive gift to be cultivated.
   b. Review briefly the other family principles of western Africa mentioned in the previous session.
      1) Stress that mutuality and interrelatedness were fundamental concepts of marriage in this culture.

2) Touch on how those principles which have been established during the lessons are critical to an understanding of the image of God.

5. Have the class read Mark 10:2-8. (This reading serves as review from the last lesson.)

6. Discuss aspects of western African culture in light of this passage.

   a. Begin to unearth the way in which this text speaks of sexuality as a part of the image of God (the material on "one flesh" being in Greek *mia sarx* and the implications of the word *sarx* through its very existential understandings are helpful here).
   b. Draw the parallels of the African concept of "one being" (a goal for African couples) being similar in its spirit-flesh unity, to the biblical term *mia sarx*.

7. Discuss with the class several potential problem areas of marriage (these may be placed on the chalkboard or newsprint).

   a. Discuss the question "What part does sex play in a healthy marriage?"
   b. Discuss the question "What part does trust play in a healthy marriage?"
   c. Discuss the question "What part does economics play in a healthy marriage?"
   d. Read Ephesians 5 and then discuss the question "What does headship mean to a healthy marriage?"
   e. Raise the question "What part does communication play in a healthy marriage?"
      1) Do not discuss this question immediately, but go on to a role-play exercise.
      2) This role-play exercise can be done in as many combinations as necessary.
      3) Use role play in Appendix C.
      4) Have groups of two divide themselves into "blamers," "placaters," "computers," and "distractors."
      5) Have each group role-play a situation in which a husband who does not smoke comes home from a trip and finds cigar butts in the ash tray. Then role-play a wife telling her husband that she has found unfamiliar lingerie in his briefcase.

6) Discuss the role plays with the question: "How was each participant communicated with in nonverbal ways?"

7) In this discussion, point out that "There is no, 'not communicating . . . even silence is communication . . .' all communication has three aspects: the report aspect, the command aspect, the context aspect" (Lederer and Jackson, *Mirages of Marriage,* pp. 97, 99).

8. Have the class break up into smaller groups to discuss the experience and instruct each group to formulate its own sentence prayer that relates to the experience.

9. Bring the class back together. Write the review topics on the chalkboard or newsprint:

   Marriage is a serious decision,

   Partners face many problems,

   Problems can be defused when partners realize the implications of being created in the image of God.

10. Pass out evaluations.

11. Collect evaluations.

12. Share sentence prayers of the groups.

13. Dismiss the class.

Materials used: Books—Lederer and Jackson, *Mirages of Marriage;* Andrew Billingsley, *Black Families in White America.* Journals—*The Journal of Ethnic Studies.*

Session 5: *Persons as Parents*

The problems that face black parents are manifold. Black persons face the same human emotional crises in parenting as do all people. For black parents, however, the problem is compounded by the alienation (economic, cultural, social) that is due to racism. James P. Comer and Alvin F. Poussaint, in their work *Black Child Care,* make the following assertion concerning the burden of black parenting:

> What is the basic problem that faces black parents? The responsibility of all parents is to help their children develop in a way that will equip them to function well as individuals, family members, and citizens. Parents are most able and willing to do this when they have a sense of belonging in the larger society. . . . In America, however, racist attitudes and actions deny blacks a oneness with

society. . . . Racism forces blacks to fight for the respect that whites take for granted. . . . Besides the above mentioned concerns black parents must also deal with all of the child-rearing issues that face every parent.[23]

Racism notwithstanding, positive self-image and interpersonal responsibility are goals that blacks must work toward if they are to face family problems courageously.

Objective of Session 5

Being made in the image of God is for families defined by the term "mutual subjection." In light of the problems facing black families in America, black parents need to familiarize themselves with what that "mutual subjection" means and to find out what skills must necessarily be developed if these particular problems are to be handled.

Lesson Plan

Major Concept to Be Learned
An awareness that mutual subjection (Ephesians 5:21) is powerful for building communication, making better decisions, strengthening love bonds.

Methods
Lecture, role play, brainstorming, discussion.

Procedure

1. Review Genesis 1:26-27.
   a. Encourage the class members to raise any questions that they still may have about the notion of the image of God.
   b. Review especially the concepts of maleness and femaleness as they relate to Genesis 1:26-27.
2. Have the class read together Ephesians 6:1-4.
3. Raise the question "What is parenting?"
   a. Have the class reflect on this question throughout the session.
   b. Point out that this concept is extremely important to the rest of the material to be presented in this session.
4. Present a rather detailed lecture.

    a. Begin the lecture by reviewing all the major points developed in these lessons concerning the African family.

    b. Present again the material dealing with responsibility, clear communications, decision making, and particular problems that face black parents.

5. Write "clear communication" on the chalkboard or newsprint and stress this as an important skill that needs to be developed in black families.

6. Using Appendix C role-playing data, have the class again do the same exercise, but this time the setting is a husband, wife, and child discussing why the child has been "playing hookey" from school.

    a. Discuss this exercise, pointing out the basic dynamics of listening, nonverbal communication, and the like.

    b. Also point out the dynamics that can affect this communication in black families, such as teenagers' use of black English; parental confusion about their images (how do they see themselves? as blacks? as negroes? as coloreds?); the defeatest attitude assumed by both children and adults as a result of racism.

7. Place on the chalkboard or newsprint the fourteen principles of decision making (see the lecture text).

    a. Discuss this material.

    b. Draw parallels between aspects of this material and the role play.

8. Have the class reread Ephesians 6:1-4.

    a. What does the text have to say about communication?

    b. What does the text have to say about decision making?

9. Point out, by the example of a "C.B." broadcast, how clear communication is based on mutual subjection (for there to be any dialogue via C.B., both sets must be turned on, one person must listen while the other talks, and so forth).

10. Allow the students to discuss their own feelings about communication and the process of decision making.

11. As an assignment, have students work up two lists, one for all the things that they think help communication; one for all the things that they think hurt it.

12. Hand out the evaluation sheets.

13. Collect the evaluation sheets and dismiss the class.

Lecture Text for Session 5

Being made in the image of God speaks clearly to the overall responsibility of parenting for both blacks and whites. Genesis 1:26-27 instructs us to be ourselves "male and female" in the image of God and to exercise that image by having dominion over our particular environment. The decision to parent is also the decision to exercise dominion over new life. That dominion, however, can only be seen clearly when seen as *responsible for*; parents are responsible *for* the lives of their children, but they are also responsible *to* the lives of their children.

Ephesians 6:1-4 outlines the relationship of parent and child with a great deal of care, and that care rests on the notion "Be subject one to another out of reverence for Christ." For black people, the family system becomes not a burden, but a great source of strength and encouragement when the mutual subjection of Ephesians is seen as that which takes individuals and places them in relationship, then produces a system greater than the sum of its parts.

Parents in the family system must be leaders in effecting clear communication. Parents must also be leaders in developing the channels for families to make cooperative decisions that are good for the growth of the entire family. Jan Chartier describes fourteen goals for decision making:

Family decision making is likely to be more effective when:

1. Channels of communication for all family members competent to contribute to a problem solution are open.
2. An appropriate distribution and clarity of authority is present.
3. Family members have sufficient commitment to invest time and energy in the process.
4. Sufficient and accurate information is available.
5. Differences of opinion and conflict are recognized and dealt with openly.
6. Cooperative, not win-lose, strategies are employed.
7. The process moves in an orderly progression from defining and understanding the problem to arriving at the most appropriate solution.

8. Major decisions are followed by appropriate and necessary satellite decisions (i.e., decisions which are necessary in light of a principal decision).
9. A healthy blend of cognitive and effective decision-making processes are available for children.
10. Parents practice and model effective decision-making processes for children.
11. Individuals feel assured that their personal needs will be considered and, whenever possible, met.
12. Families have arrived at a clear understanding of values, priorities, and goals.
13. Family members exhibit high self-esteem.
14. Family members learn from previous experience in decision making.[24]

Parents must communicate building a positive self-image within the family. With black families this is a particularly difficult task, as positive self-image is a lingering problem for many. Black Americans are involved in two revolutions: a revolt against being singled out as poor and a revolt against racial oppression. It is precisely this struggling for identity in black adults that produces much of the aggressive behavior in black adolescents. For this reason, healthy self-image is one of the most critical qualities for the black family to seek and acquire.

Being made in the image of God is for families to "mutually submit" to each other. In light of the problems facing the black family in America, black parents need to familiarize themselves with the profound implications of being a black parent in America and to find out what skills must be acquired to meet the challenge.

Materials used: Books—Olthuis, *I Pledge You My Troth;* Comer and Poussaint, *Black Child Care*; Billingsley, *Black Families in White America;* Bennett, *Before the Mayflower;* Satir, *Peoplemaking*. Journals—*The Journal of Ethnic Studies.* Lecture notes—*"Family Decision Making"* by Jan Chartier.

Session 6: *Children as Persons*

To the present-day black parent a knowledge of black history is essential. Even though a certain family may raise and nurture children in a positive way, children still must grow and be socialized in a world where many people still carry and transmit the scars of slavery and racism. The painful exposure to those scars can be defused if black parents are able to encourage the positive aspects of the black experience and couple the positive aspects of that experience to the positive religious ideals of being created in the image of God. When those notions are coupled, parents have made a significant step toward understanding and relating to children as persons. The words of Poussaint serve as a touchstone:

"We are not the masters or the servants of our children. We are not here to rule and control them or let them rule and control us. We want to help them learn to control themselves so that they can accomplish their goals and accept their responsibilities."[25]

Objective of Session 6

To enable the class to develop an appreciation for the fact that children are born to become persons and in so doing share with adults the fullness of being created in the image of God.

Again let me state that the curriculum is given only as an example of how one design with a goal of black family liberation would look. Each reader is encouraged to explore her or his circumstances for the ways in which materials might be developed that fit the uniqueness of one's own setting. Certainly much work must be done with education for senior citizens, and much must be done specifically with adolescents. Young single mothers require much attention, as do grandparents who now find themselves parents again, raising their children's children. The unique problems of black women are an area that church families must begin exploring very seriously. Certainly as Frances Berle points out in her article on being black and a woman,[26] women are not going to sit idly by much longer and not cry out at the pain of their double jeopardy at being female and black and the particular anguish that comes when they are forced to face at the hands of their own fathers, brothers, and lovers the oppression they have for so long experienced from whites.

This book is designed to establish the black extended family context as a way to think through liberation for blacks. When the family model is established as a way to think of human liberation, the potential is almost limitless as to the areas in which further study might ensue.

Lesson Plan

Major Concept to Be Learned

To develop an appreciation for the fact that children are born to become full persons and in so doing are full participants in the image of God.

Methods

Lecture, discussion, brainstorming.

Procedure

1. Lecture based on the material under "Lecture Text of Session 6."

2. Discussion.

   a. Relate the lecture material to particular aspects of adult-child interaction.

   b. Allow the students to review freely their own personal experiences and feelings concerning adult-child interaction.

   c. The instructor should again (as in the last session) raise the importance of black English to understanding our children.

      1. Point out that black English is not static.

      2. The basic forms as derived from western Africa do not change.

      3. Each generation, however, adds its own brand of slang to black English which widens the "generation gap."

3. Brief role-play exercise (this does not employ Appendix data). The setting: An adolescent male tries to communicate to his mother or father that his lover is pregnant. Or a young woman tries to tell her parent(s) that she is pregnant.

   a. Discuss this exercise in light of varying parent/adult communication styles.

   b. Discuss the differences and similarities in styles of handling extremely deep emotion.

4. Point out to the class that children are persons (write this on the chalkboard or newsprint if it seems helpful to do so).

     a. As persons, children need relationships that help them to grow.

     b. They too must be taught interpersonal responsibility if they are to grow into full personhood.

5. Raise the question "What is a home?"

     a. Brainstorm answers.

     b. If the class has not stated the following concepts, write them, too:

        Home is rest.

        Home is security.

        Home is comfort.

6. Point out that home is all these things to both children and adults.

     a. Point out also that conflicts between parent and child often come when parents exclude children from sharing emotional ownership of the home.

     b. Discuss parent-child home ownership.

7. When conflicts do arise, how can families effectively handle them? The following points from Robert B. Laurin's taped lecture *Conflict: A Biblical Perspective* should be stated and discussed:

     a. Conflict is the struggle against the diminishing forces of life.

       1) Sin is a diminishing force.

       2) Anything that prevents us from being what we are created to be is a diminishing force.

     b. Conflict comes when:

       1) individuals are not recognized in their uniqueness,

       2) individuals are not responsible for and responsive to other persons,

       3) individuals are not allowed to be free from the confines of community.

     c. Conflict can be creative when:

       1) it involves struggles against evil,

       2) it reflects human createdness in God's image, i.e., the struggle for wholeness.

     d. Black parents must learn the skills to weed out negative conflict such as that which is generated by ignoring the personhood of children, and must learn to participate in those conflicts which struggle against life's diminishing forces.

8. Review:
   a. Children are persons.
   b. Children are created in the image of God.
   c. Children need mutuality from parents.
   d. Black children have unique problems that must be faced if negative aspects of conflict are to be avoided.
9. Instructor may wish to take some time to sum up and review the basic principles of the course.
10. Hand out evaluation sheets (Evaluations 1 and 2) in Appendix C.
11. Collect evaluation sheets and dismiss the class.

Lecture Text for Session 6

When Europeans and Africans migrated to America, voluntarily or not, they brought many of their family traditions from the Old World. Immigrants tended to look at the new environment with expectations conditioned by the environment from which they came. Since the family is the basic unit in most societies, it is not surprising that Old World family customs tended to persist in the New World. It was from the family that one received the kind of security needed to enable one to survive in a strange environment.

The relationship patterns of western Africa are unique in both customs and procedure. These patterns are based on relationships with both the unborn and the dead. They are relationships that might seem superstitious to the Western or European observer. The uniqueness of relationships in western Africa has produced results for the family that are also unique. For example, in western Africa orphanages are rare and so are homes for the aged. Illegitimate children are seen as the children of the community. Large families are a norm, not for economic reasons but because custom dictates that the longer one's family survives, the longer survives the memory (i.e., the relationship with that deceased person), and the longer that deceased person remains alive.

The effect of the uniqueness of relationships has special bearing on the growth and socialization of children. In western Africa, children are viewed as unique persons. They are honored, cared for, protected. Their personhood is viewed as potential maturity, and the larger support system (family, clan, tribe) is obligated to prepare that child for life's rigors. For that reason painful initiation rites are believed to be absolutely essential and circumcision and clitoridectomies are performed at puberty as a symbol of that individual's cutting away from childhood. These initiation rites not only involved physical pain, they also were intended to force children to accept the pyschological pain related to maturity. The transposition of this phenomenon into black American culture is recounted by Richard Wright in his novel *Black Boy*. In that novel Wright tells of an incident where he, an adolescent, has been sent by his mother to the grocery store to buy groceries. In the process of coming home, he is beaten by a gang and loses his money and the groceries. When he comes home, his mother refuses to let him in the door; but gives him a big heavy stick, more grocery money, and tells him to go back to that same grocery store, and this time, to bring the groceries home. For Wright, this was a painful but practical initiation, making him aware of the necessities for survival in a violent world.

Often the transposition of the western African concept of relationships has been a tragic but practical means whereby black parents and black extended families have prepared children to face the pains of racism. One tradition which developed during slavery was for parents early in the child's life (somewhere around two years of age or at about the first sign of defiance) to beat the child severely to make sure that it would not grow up with a trace of aggressiveness, as aggressiveness in blacks potentially could bring the retribution of mutilation, torture, or death.

Materials used: Books—Olthuis, *I Pledge You My Troth;* Barnhouse and Holmes, *Male and Female;* Virginia Satir, *Peoplemaking*; Robert C. Williams, *Marriage and Family Relations;* Comer and Poussaint, *Black Child Care.* Taped material—Robert B. Laurin, *Conflict: A Biblical Perspective.*

Appendix C

Curriculum Aids

Evaluation 1

Questions used for Sessions 1 through 6.

Answer the following questions honestly and openly.

1. What did you like best about the session?
2. What did you like least about the session?
3. What from the session will be the most useful to you?
4. What did you learn from the session today?
5. What specific things came up today that you would have liked to explore further?

The following are Question 6 for each of the six sessions.

Session 1: What does it mean to be created in the image of God?

Session 2: What does being a person made in the image of God mean to you?

Session 3: How is the relationship of males and females important to a strong family?

Session 4: What problems face you in marriage, as you contemplate marriage, or as you reflect on marriage?

Session 5: What did mutual subjection in Ephesians 6:1-4 teach you about skills that are helpful for family enrichment?

Session 6: From this session what realizations about children have come to you?

Evaluation 2

Having completed this course on black family enrichment, respond to the following questions. Answers should be honest assessments of the curriculum and how you, as an individual, felt in response to the curriculum.

1. How well did you like the course?
   Excellent 5 4 3 2 1 Poor

2. Were the purposes of the course clear?
   Very clear 5 4 3 2 1 Not clear

3. How well did the group learn together?
   Very well 5 4 3 2 1 Poorly

4. How did you feel as a member of the class?
   Accepted 5 4 3 2 1 Rejected

5. How did you feel the subject matter was presented?
   Very well 5 4 3 2 1 Poorly

6. How did you feel about participating in the discussion?
   Very Free 5 4 3 2 1 Very inhibited

7. How interested were you in the topic?
   Very interested 5 4 3 2 1 Not at all interested

8. Did you gain any new insights or ideas about family enrichment?
   Many 5 4 3 2 1 None

9. How suitable was the method of teaching?
   Very suitable 5 4 3 2 1 Not at all suitable

10. How relaxed did you feel?
    Completely relaxed 5 4 3 2 1 Extremely tense

Role-Play Exercise

(adapted from Virginia Satir, *Peoplemaking,* p. 80)

1. Instructor should get three volunteers for the exercise. (Selecting participants may be necessary if some show a reluctance to get involved.)

2. Four types of communication will be employed: "placating," "blaming," "computing," and "distracting."

3. Cards may be made to give to each participant. One side of the card may contain the information on each style of communication; the other side may contain a description or picture of the posture of that communication.

4. The information on the cards will be as follows:

  a. Placater: a placater is one whose—

Words	agree. "Whatever you want is okay. I am here to make you happy."
Body	placates. "I am helpless."
Insides	say, "I feel like a nothing; without her or him I am dead. I am worthless."

Suggestions—The placater always talks in an ingratiating way, trying to please, apologizing, never disagreeing. He is a "yes man." He feels like he is nothing.

Posture—Down on one knee, one hand stretched upward (a typical begging position), head tilted back to look up for favors.

  b. Blamer: a blamer is one whose—

Words	disagree. "You never do anything right. What is the matter with you?"
Body	blames. "I am the boss around here."
Insides	say, "I am lonely and unsuccessful."

Suggestions—The blamer is a fault finder, a dictator, a boss. He acts superior, and he seems to be saying, "If it weren't for you everything would be all right." Good blaming requires you to be as loud and tyrannical as you can.

Posture—Standing, one hand on hip, the other arm extended with index finger pointed straight out. Face is screwed up, lips curled, nostrils flared.

  c. Computer: a computer is one whose—

Words	are ultra reasonable. "If one were to observe carefully one might notice the workworn hands of someone present here."

Body   computes. "I'm calm, cool, and collected."

Insides   say, "I feel vulnerable."

Suggestions—The computer is very correct, very reasonable, with no semblance of any feeling showing. He is calm, cool, and collected. He could be compared to an actual computer or a dictionary. The voice is a dry monotone, the words are apt to be abstract. Computers tend to use the longest words possible, even if they are not sure of their meaning.

Posture—The computer should sit stiffly, practically motionless; the spine should be like a stiff steel rod. The head should be tilted slightly backward. The face should be in the range of smug to expressionless.

d. Distractor: a distractor is one whose—

Words   are irrelevant.

Body   is angular and off somewhere else.

Insides   say, "Nobody cares. There is no place for me."

Suggestions—Whatever the distractor does or says is irrelevant to what anyone else is saying or doing. He never makes a response to the point. His internal feeling is one of dizziness.

Posture—The body is going in different directions at once. Knees are together in an exaggerated knock-kneed posture, buttocks stuck out. Shoulders hunched, arms and hands going in opposite directions.

Graph I
This is a diagram of the basic elements in which black Americans live. Place on
this graph feelings that you have about each sphere.

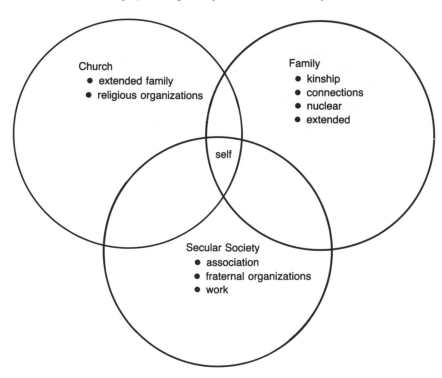

Appendix D

Chester Community
Improvement Project Outline

Introduction

The Chester Community Improvement Project (CCIP) is an organization that believes that one starting point for rehabilitating the broken communities of our nation is for citizens to come together and through personal initiative rebuild their torn-down neighborhoods. Our slogan is "People Building a Better Chester."

This specific proposal is an outline of a viable strategy to help marginalized people in Chester become homeowners through securing and rehabilitating some of Chester's numerous abandoned houses. The purpose of this program is to show that if people are given a chance to own their own homes, they will have a much better chance of overcoming the negative self-images and feelings of worthlessness that spring out of living in ravaged, run-down communities.

The implementation of this program rests on the following assumptions:

First, the abandoned housing stock in Chester provides an ideal starting point for people to begin rebuilding communities. Through the newly established process of judicial sales, abandoned houses can be purchased at tax delinquent sales for a minimum bid of $600. This sale eradicates all liens and encumbrances from the sought-after properties.

Second, the geographical integrity of the neighborhood is important. Implementing the program by securing a large number of homes in an already existing neighborhood where

147

there are some stable family dwellings and established churches provides for the incoming residents a sense of stability and
belonging rather than isolation and abandonment. The program would have to seek the total support of the existing
churches and residents in the target geographical area to act
as full partners in the process of community rebuilding.

Third, one of the things that stands in the way of persons
doing a program such as this on their own is the bureaucratic
"red tape" involved and the fact that marginalized persons
often do not have access to the information necessary to begin
such an undertaking. CCIP would provide through local community volunteers and volunteer students from area colleges
such as Swarthmore College a corps of people who whould dis-
seminate information and cut through "red tape."

Fourth, such a program, once in operation, would provide
through the newly rebuilt community a chance for political
and economic strength which ultimately is the bottom line for
ongoing social change in contexts of oppression.

Fifth, community involvement which is critical for success
would be secured on an ongoing basis through the participation
of each new homeowner on the board of CCIP.

Sixth, the overall goal of securing a large number of homes
in a geographical area must be accomplished through a gradual
program of more manageable objectives, involving work on
several houses at a time in target blocks within the larger
target neighborhood.

Overview

The goal of the CCIP Housing Rehabilitation Project is to
acquire and rehabilitate abandoned properties in Chester and
sell them to low- and moderate-income families. The homes are
acquired as tax delinquent properties from the Tax Claim Bureau of Delaware County for a minimal cost (less than $600 in
most cases). The homes are rehabilitated by qualified contractors and local community people volunteering their skills and
time. Since most of the labor is done by volunteers, the primary
cost of the rehabilitation work to CCIP is for materials. This
cost is between six and ten thousand dollars for each house.
The homes are sold at cost (acquisition, rehabilitation, and
holding costs) to qualified families. Each participating family
is required to assist in the rehabilitation work on its own des-

ignated property. With the sale of the home, the money that CCIP receives is put into another property and the process starts again.

In the first phase of the project CCIP purchased up to ten abandoned homes in a specific area. Six of these homes are located on one block. With the homes in a concentrated area, CCIP hopes to maximize the effect the rehabilitated homes will have on the neighborhood and facilitate the building of an improved community in this depressed area. As homes are completed, CCIP will move into adjacent blocks in the target area.

Location of Properties

CCIP chose to begin its work on a block of West Second Street between Broomall and Lamokin Streets because of the block's proximity to the CCIP office and the character of the block. Eight homes on the block have recently been improved by their owners. In an on-sight inspection by CCIP technical consultants, six of the ten abandoned properties on the block were found to be structurally sound for rehabilitation.

There are two ways that CCIP purchases abandoned properties from Delaware County: private sale and county judicial sale. In a private sale, CCIP makes a written bid to the county for a property which has already gone through a tax upset sale. If the bid is accepted by the county, city, and school board solicitors, then CCIP receives deed to the property, with the owed taxes being written off but all liens remaining.

In a county judicial sale, which is held at intervals over the year, CCIP can place properties on the judicial sale list if they have gone through a tax upset sale. In the actual sale, CCIP must verbally bid on the properties in competition with other bidders. A minimum bid of $600 is required. In contrast to the private sale, all owed taxes and liens are written off. Hence, it is the amount of liens on the property which determine the process by which CCIP attempts to acquire the property.

In each process, CCIP is able to acquire the homes for under $1,100, including settlement costs and title insurance.

Family Selection Process

CCIP maintains contact with area residents through neighborhood and church meetings. In this way, CCIP meets or speaks with interested families. Families must do the following to participate in the CCIP Housing Rehabilitation Project.

1. Take part in a home interview with a CCIP representative.
2. Take part in a follow-up interview with the CCIP Family Selection Committee of the CCIP Board.
3. Meet CCIP's financial guidelines, which are variable according to the cost of the property, the estimated operating cost of the property, and the family situation. It is assumed that participating families will be taking a loan from an area bank in order to purchase the home from CCIP. CCIP would like the monthly mortgage payments not to exceed 25 percent of a family's monthly income. Total outstanding debts should not exceed 36 percent of income. Families should have a good credit rating or special circumstances to explain a less than perfect credit rating. (These criteria are based on the requirements of the Chester Mortgage Plan.)

To aid the families in determining whether owning a certain home is affordable, CCIP provides a project budget for each home. This includes the estimated acquisition and rehabilitation cost of the property. This is the amount that the family needs to purchase the property from CCIP. In addition, the project budget includes an estimated yearly operating cost for the property.

Since most of the families involved in the project are first-time homeowners, CCIP provides extensive home-ownership counseling. By looking at the estimated yearly operating cost, the families are able to see in advance what their financial situation and responsibilities will be.

CCIP Agreement with Participating Families

At or shortly after the purchase of the property by CCIP, an agreement of sale is executed between CCIP and the designated family. This contract provides for the sale of the home by CCIP to the purchaser at a cost which is presumably well below market cost. The cost will vary with each home. The cost includes all acquisition costs for the property, all renovation and rehabilitation costs, and any holding costs such as insurance which CCIP needed to pay. CCIP estimates the cost of most of the homes in the project to be between six and ten thousand dollars.

The agreement of sale also includes a number of provisions by which CCIP hopes to ensure that each property sold adds to the improvement of the community. The family agrees to take an active role in the rehabilitation of the property by volunteering time to participate in the rehabilitation work, particularly in the cosmetic phase which includes painting, plastering, and some carpentry. If the family wishes to sell the property anytime in the first three years, they must first offer the property back to CCIP at the original cost plus settlement costs. The property cannot be used for commercial purposes. It must be owner-occupied and cannot be used for rental purposes. The purchaser also agrees to maintain the home and the property surrounding it. Some of these restrictions will also be listed on the deed to the property.

This agreement of sale is pursuant to the purchaser obtaining the necessary financing from a lending institution. This can be either through a loan pool set up for CCIP by an area bank or through any bank of their choice.

Rehabilitation Work

Once title to the property is obtained by CCIP, the actual rehabilitation work can start. CCIP will take out the necessary insurance for the duration of the work. Members of the CCIP Board, who are qualified and experienced in rehabilitation work, supervise each project. A number of local contractors (electricians, plumbers, and carpenters) volunteer their skills to work on aspects of the rehabilitation. Using volunteers from local church and community groups in addition to local college students, the contractors are provided with helpers during the course of the work. CCIP purchases all the necessary materials. Materials should be purchased at wholesale or below cost from area businesses. (They can receive a tax credit for donations to the project because of CCIP's nonprofit [501-3-c] status.)

The work follows as closely as possible the project budget, though CCIP realizes that some cost overruns may occur. Presumably, most homes will need extensive electrical work, plumbing overhauls, roof repairs, air and water heater installation, and window/door installation. This work is outlined in the project budget. Particular homes may need additional work resulting from the lack of maintenance, i.e. porch repairs, masonry, and other miscellaneous carpentry repairs. A security system is set up to make sure that the properties are not vandalized during the rehabilitation period.

Once the rehabilitation work is completed in accordance with the project budget, CCIP makes settlement with the purchaser, persuant to the terms of the already executed agreement of sale. At this time, CCIP will be reimbursed its acquisition, rehabilitation, and holding costs. CCIP will then put the money back into another property and the cycle will continue.

CCIP Office and Community Center

CCIP is presently seeking funds from area foundations and corporations to purchase and rehabilitate an abandoned home in our target area to be used as an office and community center. CCIP proposes to set up a tool bank and resource library for use by all community residents. Courses would be offered in home improvements, such as plumbing, electrical work, and carpentry. This would be an important support program for the housing rehabilitation project, enabling the new homeowners to learn basic home maintenance skills. In addition, the center would serve as an information source for the community in all aspects of rehabilitation and home improvement.

Conclusion

With the successful completion of a number of homes on West Second Street between Broomall and Lamokin Streets, CCIP will move its program to blocks adjacent to the 1200 block of West Second Street. In this manner, CCIP will gradually improve the six-block area surrounding the original target area. CCIP is presently seeking to expand the housing rehabilitation program and to implement new community building programs. There is also the possiblity of CCIP working as an advocate for issues important to the community in that area.

Notes

Introduction

[1] J. Deotis Roberts, *Roots of a Black Future: Family and Church* (Philadelphia: The Westminster Press, 1980), p. 132.

[2] C. L. Franklin, Chicago, Ill.: Chess Records, n.d.

[3] James Cone, *The God of the Oppressed* (New York: Seabury Press, 1975), p. 108. In this book Cone gives a very detailed explanation of the history behind the arguments of Christology from above or below. Christology from above is basically the variety that focuses on the cosmic kingliness of Jesus Christ. Christology from below centers more on the experience of the historical Jesus. It is an oversimplification to say that blacks opted for the "below" approach. Blacks never would have been comfortable with the reason over revelation dimensions that this school has taken. It is fairly safe to say that the Rudolph Bultmans of the world who through reason attempt to demythologize Scripture would find no home in most black churches in America.

[4] "Great Day, Great Day" from *The New National Baptist Hymnal* (Nashville, Tenn.: National Baptist Publishing Board, 1977), no. 508.

Chapter 1

[1] This question has been raised time and time again and is dealt with in large measure by the infamous Moynihan Report of 1965. The argument for matriarchy is bankrupt for two reasons. First, it is an argument totally out of touch with the economic realities that force families into abhorrent patterns. Secondly, the equality of black women was forced upon the black slave female. Male and female in slavery suffered equally. The tender treatment white males gave to white females was something never extended by the master to slave women. Angela Davis, in her book *Women Class and Race* (Harper and Row, 1983), points out that the black male slave and the black female slave were partners in agony. There was no sexual difference or deference expressed to slave women.

[2] E. Franklin Frazier, in his classic 1934 work *The Black Family,* held the thesis that the traditions of Africa did not survive the middle passage and that

153

present-day Negro culture was an expression of white culture assimilated by blacks through slavery.

[3] Melville Herskovits, in his landmark work *The Myth of the Negro Past* (Boston: Beacon Press, 1958), was one of the first to use rigorous scholarship to take exception with Frazier and establish that certain customs and practices of black Americans were a result of African retentions.

[4] Angela Davis, in *Women Class and Race,* also raises the issue that the image of black women is not really understood by black males or whites. She mentions that the parameters of the confusion have on one side the white myth of Aunt Jemima, the big jolly mother figure. On the other side is the black male stereotype of the woman as noble help-mate to her fallen warrior companion. Indeed, much work must be done to discover the authentic image of the black woman.

[5] Individually commissioned studies have appeared through the NAACP and the Urban League. Dr. J. Deotis Roberts, in an unpublished address, responded to these studies from the perspective of the black church. His thesis was that these studies have by and large ignored the fact that there continues to be stability in those families which are in the church. Interview with J. D. Roberts, Eastern Baptist Theological Seminary, Philadelphia, Pa., April 1984.

[6] It cannot be stated forcibly enough that the problems faced by the black family are a result of the economic hardships faced by blacks as a result of racism. Jerry M. Lewis and John G. Looney, in *the Long Struggle,* surveyed eighteen black families and made the following conclusions: "Nevertheless, it is important to emphasize that each of the three families with incomes below their size-adjusted poverty levels was seen as less competent. The demographic data underscore the importance of economic factors in discriminating the two groups." Jerry Lewis and John G. Looney, *The Long Struggle: Well-Functioning Working-Class Black Families* (New York: Brunner Mazel, 1983), pp. 52-53.

[7] In a doctoral dissertation at Bryn Mawr College, Ann Jenkins, in studying the churches of Chester, a Pennsylvania industrial city of fifty thousand, reports that the persons generally under the national median income level were the persons primarily outside of the organized church structure. Ann Jenkins, "Leadership in a Black Community: A Model for the Study of Urban Communities" (Ph. D. dissertation, Bryn Mawr College, 1984).

[8] Myron R. Chartier, "The Nature and Mission of the Church," unpublished paper prepared for Faculty Theological Colloquium at Eastern Baptist Theological Seminary, December 5, 1980, p. 1.

[9] *Ibid.,* p. 2.

[10] C. Eric Lincoln, *Before the Mayflower: A History of the Negro in America* (Chicago: Johnson Publication Company, 1964), pp. 30-31.

[11] John Herbers, "Income Gap Between Races Wide as in 1960, Study Finds," *New York Times,* July 18, 1983.

[12] Melville Herskovits, in *Myth of the Negro Past,* points out that the slaves used family titles such as "uncle" and "aunt" as a sign of deep respect. This was one way that the black family was, through the creation of an extended network, dealing with the way the nuclear family was being decimated (Boston: Beacon Press, 1958), p. 150.

[13] See Herbert G. Gutmann, *The Black Family in Slavery and Freedom*

(New York: Pantheon Books, 1976).

Chapter 2

[1] Niara Suderkasa, "Interpreting the Afro-American Heritage in the Afro-American Family Organization" in *Black Families,* ed., Harriet McAdoo (London: Sage, 1981), p. 40.

[2] *Ibid.,* p. 41.

[3] *Ibid.*

[4] *Ibid.*

[5] *Ibid.,* p. 43.

[6] *Ibid.,* p. 44.

[7] C. Eric Lincoln, *Before the Mayflower: A History of the Negro in America* (Chicago: Johnson Publishing Company, 1964), pp. 30-31.

[8] Robert C. Williamson, *Marriage and Family Relations* (New York: John Wiley and Sons, 1972), p. 81.

[9] *Ibid.,* p. 82.

[10] Jean Nobels, "Status of the Black American Woman" in *World Encyclopedia of Black People* (St. Clair Shores, Michigan: Scholarly Press, 1975), p. 144.

[11] Jualynne Dodson, "Conceptualizations of Black Families" in *Black Families,* ed., Harriet McAdoo (London: Sage, 1981), p. 24.

[12] *Ibid.,* p. 24

[13] *Ibid.*

[14] J. Deotis Roberts, *Roots of a Black Future: Family and Church* (Philadelphia: The Westminster Press, 1980), p. 24.

[15] Melville Herskovits, *Myth of the Negro Past.* The entire thesis put forth by Herskovits is based on the contention that African retentions do exist in the new world. The thesis is a controversial one but in essence is the progenitor of much of the thinking which constitutes contemporary black theology.

[16] Jualynne Dodson, *Black Families,* p. 27.

[17] *Ibid.,* p. 29.

[18] In Rose Laub Coser, *The Family: Its Structure and Functions* (New York: St. Martins Press, 1974), pp. 579-580.

[19] Harry A. Ploski and Ernest Kaiser, *Afro USA* (New York: Belwether Publishing, 1967), p. 375.

[20] Charles V. Willie, *The Family Life of Black People* (Columbus, Ohio: Charles E. Merrill, 1970), p. 316.

[21] In Arlene S. Skolnick and James H. Skolnick, *Family in Transition: Rethinking Marriage, Sexuality, Child Rearing and Family Organization* (Boston: Little, Brown and Company, 1971), p. 397.

[22] Willie, *The Family Life of Black People,* p. 294.

[23] Skolnick and Skolnick, *Family in Transition,* p. 3.

[24] *Ibid.*

[25] *Ibid.,* p. 404.

[26] *Ibid.*, p. 419.

[27] *Ibid.*, p. 430.

[28] *Ibid.*

Chapter 3

[1] Cornell West, *Prophesy Deliverance! An Afro-American Revolutionary Christianity* (Philadelphia: The Westminster Press, 1982), p. 22.

[2] *Ibid.*, p. 53.

[3] *Ibid.*, p. 54.

[4] *Ibid.*, p. 55.

[5] West's articulation of these historical realities (beginning on page 53 of his book) is an outstanding treatment and bears a great deal more reflection and research as an area where the church must concentrate energy and influence to correct the centuries of this proliferation of misinformation.

[6] *Ibid.*, p. 62.

[7] Karl Barth, *Church Dogmatics* (Edinborough: T. T. Clark, 1961), p. 116.

[8] *Ibid.*

[9] *Ibid.*, p. 117.

[10] Genesis 1:26-27 and the notion of self-image were chosen for detailed analysis in this paper because of the author's deep personal feeling about the criticalness of individual positive self-image for personal wholeness. Other possible ways to develop the self-image concept might have been through an examination of the latest developments in the interpretations of the *Song of Songs,* particularly Marvin Pope's work in the *Anchor Bible.* Pope hits the self-image problem directly when he translates chapter 1, verse 5 as "Black and I am beautiful" (William Foxwell Albright and David Noel Freedman, gen. eds., *The Anchor Bible,* 58 vols. [New York: Doubleday and Co., 1964], vol. 7c: Song of Songs, by Marvin Pope [1977], p. 1), an affirmation which blacks popularized in the 1960s. Pope's work points to the fact that the concept of black self-worth is supported by ancient biblical material. This affirmation is extremely important in light of the specious scholarship that allowed positive black self-image to be abjured for centuries through the "curse of Ham" view.

[11] Wallace C. Smith, "A Family Enrichment Curriculum for the Black Church," D.Min. thesis project, Eastern Baptist Theological Seminary, 1979, p. 12.

[12] *Ibid.*, p. 22.

[13] Gerrit Berkouwer, *Man: The Image of God* (Grand Rapids: Wm. B. Eerdmans, 1962), p. 9.

[14] Samuel Rolles Driver, Alfred Plumer, and Charles Augustus Briggs, gen. eds., *The International Critical Commentary, 40 volumes* (New York: Charles Scribner, 1910), vol. 17, *Genesis,* by John Skinner, p. 32.

[15] Jean Paul Sartre, *Being and Nothingness* (New York: Washington Square Press, 1966), p. 9.

[16] *Ibid.*

[17] Frank Stagg, *Polarities of Man's Existence in Biblical Perspective* (Philadelphia: The Westminster Press, 1952), p. 45.

[18] *Ibid.*, p. 48.

[19] *Ibid.*, p. 58.

[20] *Ibid.*, p. 59.

[21] *Ibid.*, pp. 59-60.

[22] John Calvin, *Institutes of the Christian Religion, vol. 1,* trans. Henry Beveridge (Grand Rapids: Wm. B. Eerdmans, 1957), p. 38.

[23] Berkouwer, *Man: The Image of God,* p. 21.

[24] Eric Brunner, *Man in Revolt,* (Philadelphia: The Westminster Press, 1957), p. 19.

[25] Brunner, *Man in Revolt,* p. 92.

[26] *Ibid.*

[27] Gerhard von Rad, *Genesis: A Commentary* (Philadelphia: The Westminster Press, 1965), p. 57.

[28] C. F. D. Moule, *Man and Nature in the New Testament* (London: Athlone Press, 1964), p. 5.

[29] *Ibid.*, p. 5.

[30] Stagg, *Polarities of Man's Existence,* p. 53.

[31] *Ibid.*

[32] *Ibid.*, p. 39.

[33] von Rad, *Genesis,* p. 58.

[34] Brunner, *Man in Revolt,* p. 345.

[35] *Ibid.*, p. 346.

[36] Stagg, *Polarities of Man's Existence,* pp. 75, 77.

[37] *Ibid.*, p. 76.

Chapter 4

[1] Jualynne Dodson, "Conceptualizations of Black Families" in *Black Families,* ed., Harriet McAdoo (London: Sage, 1981), p. 29.

[2] Elmer P. Martin and Joanne Mitchell Martin, *The Black Extended Family* (Chicago: University of Chicago Press, 1978), p. 114.

[3] *Ibid.*, p. 6.

[4] *Ibid.*, p. 9.

[5] *Ibid.*, p. 39.

[6] *Ibid.*, p. 41.

[7] Markus Barth, trans. and ed., "Ephesians" of *The Anchor Bible,* ed. William Foxwell Albright and David Noel Freedman (Garden City: Doubleday and Company, Inc., 1974). pp. 661-662. Reprinted by permission of the publishers.

[8] *Ibid.*, p. 608.

[9] *Ibid.*

[10] *Ibid.*

[11] *Ibid.*, p. 613.

[12] *Ibid.*

[13] *Ibid.*. For further discussion see pp. 613-614.

[14]*Ibid.*, p. 607.

[15]Heinrich Schlier, "KEQVN" in *The Theological Dictionary of the New Testament,* ed., Gerhard Kittel, vol. 3 (Grand Rapids: Wm. B. Eerdmans, 1966), p. 680.

[16]*Ibid.*, p. 613.

[17]Andrew Billingsley, *Black Families in White America* (Englewood Cliffs, N.J.: Prentice-Hall, 1968), p. 40. Reprinted by permission of the publishers.

[18]Paul K. Jewett, *Man As Male and Female* (Grand Rapids: Wm. B. Eerdmans, 1975), p. 24. Used by permission.

[19]*Ibid.*, p. 13.

[20]*Ibid.*, p. 14.

[21]Quoted in L. Christenson, *The Christian Family* (Minneapolis: Bethany Fellowship, 1970), p. 9.

Chapter 5

[1]"The Church Looks for Ways to Aid Families," *The United Methodist Reporter,* December 16, 1983.

[2]J. Deotis Roberts, *Roots of a Black Future: Family and Church* (Philadelphia: The Westminster Press, 1980), p. 133.

[3]Church Service: Pastor's Twenty-fifth Anniversary, Mt. Zion Baptist Church, 50th and Woodland Aves., Philadelphia, Pa., March 11, 1984.

[4]Edward P. Wimberly, *Pastoral Care in the Black Church* (Nashville: Abingdon Press, 1979), p. 39.

[5]Church Service: Pastor's Anniversary, Mt. Zion Baptist Church, March 11, 1984.

[6]Cornell West, *Prophesy Deliverance!* (Philadelphia: The Westminster Press, 1982), pp. 47-48.

[7]Cited in Thomas B. Roberts, "Education and Transpersonal Relations: A Research Agenda," *Simulation and Games 8* (March 1977), p. 10-11.

[8]Ann Jenkins, "Leadership in a Black Community: A Model for the Study of Urban Communities," Ph.D. dissertation, Bryn Mawr College, 1984.

Chapter 6

[1]The Ham doctrine is a perfect example of a biblical hermeneutic of over-spiritualization. The contention that Ham comes from the Egyptian "Shem," meaning "servant," is spurious at best. One has to do some biblical gymnastics to equate Ham's curse with blackness. Nowhere does the biblical text say that. Only through eisegetic embellishment can that assertion be made. For an excellent treatment of this problem, see Latta Thomas, *Biblical Faith and the Black American* (Valley Forge: Judson Press, 1976).

[2]Virginia Satir, *Peoplemaking* (Palo Alto: Science and Behavior Books, Inc., 1972), p. 3.

[3]Christian education has also begun with the pulpit work of black preachers. No better example exists than Dr. Martin Luther King, Jr., who literally educated millions of blacks to the possibilities of freedom with his matchless oratory.

[4]Samuel McKinney and Floyd Massey, Jr., *Church Administration in the*

Black Perspective (Valley Forge: Judson Press, 1976).

[5] Reginald U. Stephens, term paper done in course "Issues in Black Church Ministry," Eastern Baptist Theological Seminary, 1984.

Epilogue

[1] James F. White, *Sacraments as God's Self Giving* (Nashville: Abingdon Press, 1983), p. 93.

[2] *Ibid.*, p. 94.

[3] *Ibid.*, p. 97.

[4] *Ibid.*, p. 97.

[5] Matthew Fox, *A Spirituality Named Compassion and the Healing of the Global Village: Humpty Dumpty and Us* (Minneapolis: Winston Press, 1979), p. 41. For further study see Fox's chapter on "Dancing Sarah's Circle." It raises some very good issues about the concept of sight versus hearing and the way in which hearing was foundational to the Jewish faith.

Appendix B

[1] Palo Freire, *Pedagogy of the Oppressed* (New York: Continuum Publishing Corp., 1982), p. 59.

[2] Martha M. Leypoldt, *Learning Is Change* (Valley Forge: Judson Press, 1971), p. 6.

[3] J. Cecil Parker and Louis J. Rubin, *Process as Content* (Chicago: Rand McNally and Co., 1966), p. 2.

[4] Ralph W. Tyler, *Basic Principles of Curriculum and Instruction* (Chicago: University of Chicago Press, 1950), p. 30.

[5] Thomas B. Roberts, ed., *Four Psychologies Applied to Education: Freudian, Behavioral, Humanistic, Transpersonal* (New York: Halsted Press, 1975), p. 328.

[6] Virginia Satir, *Peoplemaking* (Palo Alto: Science and Behavior Books, 1972), p. 3.

[7] Brent D. Ruben and John Kim, *General Systems Theory and Human Communication* (Rochelle Park, N.Y.: Hayden Books, 1975), p. 150.

[8] *Ibid.*

[9] *Ibid.*, p. 151.

[10] Satir, *Peoplemaking*, p. 31.

[11] Frederick S. Perls, Ralph F. Hefferline and Paul Goodman, *Gestalt Therapy: Excitement and Growth in the Human Personality* (New York: Julian Press, 1951), p. 51.

[12] Jack L. Daniel, ed., *Black Communications Dimensions of Research and Instruction* (New York: Speech Communication Association, 1974), p. 136.

[13] William J. Lederer and Don D. Jackson, *The Mirages of Marriage* (New York: W. W. Norton and Co., 1968), p. 99.

[14] Martha M. Leypoldt, *Forty Ways to Teach in Groups* (Valley Forge: Judson Press, 1967), p. 37.

[15] Frank Stagg, *Polarities of Man's Existence in Biblical Perspective* (Philadelphia: The Westminster Press, 1973), p. 75.

16 John Herbers, "Income Gap Between Races: Wide as in 1960 Study Finds," *New York Times,* July 18, 1983.

17 Frederick W. Farrar, *History of Biblical Interpretation* (New York: E. P. Dutton and Co., 1886), p. 12.

18 James Olthuis, *I Pledge You My Troth: Marriage, Family, Friendship* (New York: Harper and Row, 1975), p. 4.

19 Stagg, *Polarities of Man's Existence,* p. 5.

20 Satir, *Peoplemaking,* p. 22.

21 Lederer and Jackson, *Mirages of Marriage,* p. 87.

22 Andrew Billingsley, *Black Families in White America* (Englewood Cliffs, N.J.: Prentice-Hall, Inc., 1968), p. 28.

23 James P. Comer and Alvin F. Poussaint, eds., *Black Child Care* (New York: Simon and Schuster, 1975), p. 292.

24 Dr. Jan Chartier, material presented in a lecture given at Eastern Baptist Seminary, Philadelphia, Pa., January 10, 1974.

25 Comer and Poussaint, *Black Child Care,* p. 292.

26 Frances Berle in *Black Theology: A Documentary History 1966-1979,* Gayraud Wilmore and James Core, eds. (New York: Orbis Books, 1979), p. 368.

Other References for Appendix B

Barnhouse and Holmes, *Male and Female: Christian Approaches to Sexuality* (New York: The Seabury Press, Inc., 1976).

C. Eric Lincoln, *Before the Mayflower: A History of Black America* (Chicago: Johnson Publishing, Co., Inc., 1964.)

Jan Chartier, "Family Decision Making" (lecture notes).

Journal of Ethnic Studies.

Robert B. Laurin, *"Conflict: A Biblical Perspective" (taped material).*

Robert C. Williamson, *Marriage and Family Relations* (New York: John Wiley and Sons, 1972).